African Muslims
in Antebellum America

بسم الله الرحمن الرحيم

In the name of God, the merciful ! the compassionate ! God bless our Lord Mohammed his prophet, and his descendants, and his followers, and prosper them exceedingly. Praise be to God the Lord of all creatures ! the merciful, the compassionate king of the day of judgment ! Thee we adore, and of thee we implore assistance ! Guide us in the right way, the way of those with whom thou art well pleased, and not of those with whom thou art angry, nor of those who are in error. Amen!

The Fatiha, the Opening *Surah* of the Quran, Islam's First Prayer, of Charno [Chierno] and Translation, Georgia, c. 1830.

African Muslims in Antebellum America

Transatlantic Stories and Spiritual Struggles

Allan D. Austin

ROUTLEDGE
New York and London

Published in 1997 by

Routledge
29 West 35th Street
New York, NY 10001

Published in Great Britain in 1997 by

Routledge
11 New Fetter Lane
London EC4P 4EE

Printed in the United States of America
Design: Jack Donner

Library of Congress Cataloging-in-Publication Data

African Muslims in antebellum America : Transatlantic stories and spiritual struggles
Allan D. Austin. — [Rev. and updated ed.]
p.   cm.
Originally published: Garland Pub., 1984, in series:
Critical studies on black life and culture; v. 5
ISBN 0–415–91269–5 (hard: alk. paper)
ISBN 0–415–91270–9 (pbk.: alk. paper)
1. Slaves—United States—Biography.   2. Afro-Americans—History—To 1863—Sources.   3.
Muslims—United States—History—Sources.   4. Slavery—United States—History—Sources.
5. Slaves—America—Biography.   6. Slavery—America—History—Sources.
7. Muslims—America—History—Sources.
E444.A25   1996
973'.0496—dc 20   96–31876
CIP

Contents

Acknowledgments

Early on in the original version of this project—the one I began in the late 1970s thinking it might lead to an article—my mentor and the collector of the widest range of information on African Americans, the late Prof. Sidney Kaplan of the University of Massachusetts, Amherst, introduced me to several of the minor African Muslim figures to add to those with whom I was already familiar. The most productive and generous correspondent was Prof. Thomas C. Parramore of Raleigh, North Carolina, who knew more about Umar ibn Said and his writings than anyone else. Parramore also introduced me to papers on Osman and S'Quash. Mary C. Beaty, the reference librarian at the Davidson College Library in Davidson, North Carolina, provided further documents on and a portrait of Umar. Sylvia Lara of the University of Cantinas in São Paulo, Brazil, told me about Mahommah Baquaqua making it to England.

Original translations of manuscripts in Arabic were provided by three busy men: Dr. Elias Saad, scholar interested in fellow scholars from Timbuktu to Baghdad and beyond, Wellesley, Massachusetts; my good friend and Muslim source of inspiration, Dr. Kamal Ali, Westfield State University, Westfield, Massachusetts; and Dr. Abdullah Basabrian, graduate student at the University of Massachusetts, Amherst, in the early 1980s, now somewhere in Saudi Arabia. The recent polisher of these early translations, Muhammad al-Ahari, Chicago, an indefatigable tracer of lost Muslims, has brought several corrections and additions to this book.

Because I submitted an acknowledgments page too early to the first version of the stories that follow, my *African Muslims in Antebellum America: A Sourcebook* (New York: Garland, 1984), I herewith want to belatedly thank my staff—a sort of revolving one, as I remember—of copyeditors eventually under the eye of Phyllis Korper, who made my first collection of old papers, notes, introductions, and photographs into a book.

I want now to thank Marlie Wasserman, who brought my manuscript to Routledge and gave me some much-needed early guidance, and Connie Oehring, whose precise copyediting has corrected and streamlined my ponderous prose.

I thank you one and all.

Finally, I want also to express my appreciation first to my Humanities Department and the faculty members who approved and Vice President Malvina Rau who authorized a sabbatical year from my academic home, Springfield College, Springfield, Massachusetts; and second to those enthusiastic and wide-ranging scholars Henry Louis Gates, Jr., Richard Newman, and Randall Burkett at the W. E. B. Du Bois Institute for Afro-American Research at Harvard University, where I spent 1994–1995; and, most emphatically, to my wife, Joyce, for financing out of her business that sabbatical year and for staying with me through my several announcements that I was just about finished with the sometimes tortuous extracting and bridging of the original *African Muslims in Antebellum America.*

Preface

This book is a radical condensation of my *African Muslims in Antebellum America: A Sourcebook* (New York: Garland, 1984), an illustrated collection of the majority of then-available documents accompanied by introductions and extensive notes. It is also an update including short notices of about forty more people, four manuscripts in Arabic, a portrait, and scholarship discovered since 1984. It reprints five of six maps but has thirteen fewer illustrations. Instead of notes and a bibliography, I have provided a Selected Reading list at the end of each chapter. In nearly all cases, the original documents and citations from obscure sources may be found in my earlier book.

Some names of major figures are changed here. I continue to use the familiar Job Ben Solomon, but I have changed Abdul Rahahman to Abd ar-Rahman, because this is the way he pronounced his name to his earliest interviewers and it is closer to an Arabic standard; Lamen Kebe to Lamine Kebe, because contemporary writers were not sure how to pronounce the name and the latter pronunciation better approaches the Serahule standard; and Omar to Umar, because contemporaries heard different pronunciations and Umar is closer to the Arabic standard. I discuss the pronunciation of Bilali in Chapter 5.

Maps and Illustrations

African Muslims
in Antebellum America

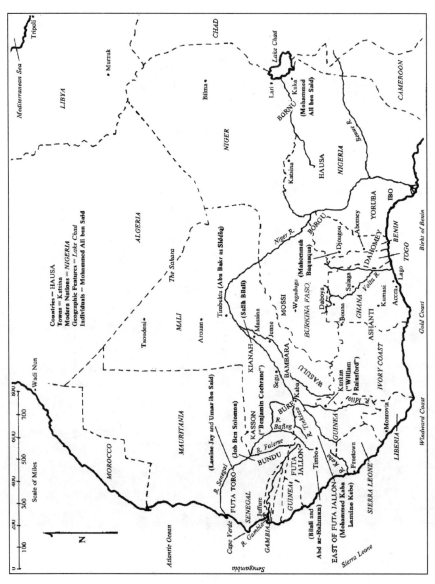

Map 1. The Homelands.

1

"There Are Good Men in America, but All Are Very Ignorant of Africa" —and Its Muslims

"There are good men in America, but all are very ignorant of Africa," declared the African-born Lamine Kebe in 1835, after forty years of American slavery in three Southern states. Kebe might also have said, "and very ignorant of Islam in both Africa and America." Criticisms, recollections, and stories by and about Old World immigrants and the ways they reacted to and changed the New World after 1492 have been told and retold throughout the centuries. Stories have differed, of course, with the teller, beginning with the Native Americans, Spanish, French, British, Dutch, or the Africans these four European nations brought with them. Stories told by those who arrived later—Swedes, Irish, Germans, Italians, Chinese, Jews, Arabs, Latin Americans, and Southeast Asians—have also varied considerably, as do those by males and females, rich and poor, free and indentured or enslaved, and Christians and non-Christians. Stories by African immigrants, including those who were, like Kebe, Muslims, have been fewer for many reasons that I will explore later. Here the emphasis is on stories by African Muslims—a proud people, influential beyond their numbers on both sides of the Atlantic Ocean—who until very recently had been almost completely neglected by modern America's eagle-eyed historians and storytellers.

It is a fact, of course, that most African Muslims, like the great majority of the first Africans in America, remain anonymous or are little more than names

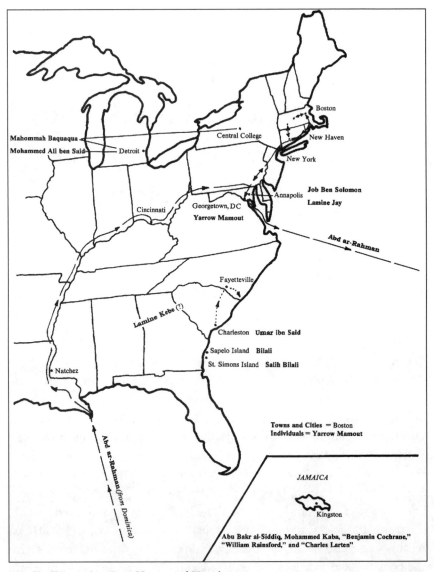

Map II. Known American Homes and Travels.

in slave-property lists. Their individual arrivals appeared in no public records, and no accounts of sales from slave ships have survived. Very few were allowed to go to school, to own property, to marry, to go to court, or to have their deaths legally recorded or probated. Africans and their children in America have always been of interest, of course, as laboring property, strangers, exotics, threats, and, in the Constitution, as discounted, disenfranchised persons—each three-fifths of a white male—used in yet another way to strengthen the voting power of slaveholders. But those who wanted African slaves could not or dared not concern themselves with Muslim or non-Muslim cultural and moral acquisitions over their need to get a return on their investments, to get their crops in, or to get their parlor doors open or closed. Few could look into such moral contradictions as the enslavement of literate people who were monotheistic and familiar with Biblical figures, even though such knowledge was supposed to be honored by Christians above all others except, perhaps, making money. Most slaveholders had to suppress manifestations of non-Christian religious practices that might be used to unite or direct their slaves. If necessary, they found some way to accommodate the proudest people by recognizing and rewarding a supposedly exceptional slave with limited power over others. All masters had to oppose the distribution of letters in a language they could not read. Accordingly, those who wrote about the people considered in this book were very careful about how much they told and whom they told.

Despite such practical considerations, however, much evidence of the Muslim presence has survived. Lists of slaves include Muslim names. Some family and church documents, including birth and death notices of slaves, add an occasional informative note; runaway advertisements provide useful descriptive information; and some slaves became worthy of notice in print for a variety of reasons. Seventy-five African-born Muslims who were brought to North America between 1730 and 1860—several literate in Arabic—are discussed in this book. Maps I and II point out African homelands and American homes respectively.

Stories about some of these African Muslims may appear to be fantastic, but collateral sources corroborate each narrative. The protagonists were often the tellers; their stories are instructive and touching on several levels. Eight inspired respectable attention from people with access to printers.

Chapter 3 discusses the earliest known "life and thoughts" of an African who had been a slave in the New World. The fifty-four-page *Some Memoirs of the Life of Job Ben Solomon* (1734), the oldest text in African American literature, is about a runaway in Maryland, a proud historian of his religion and country to the nobility and intelligentsia in England, and a wealthy returnee to the country now called Senegal. It is a very respectable and self-respecting piece written by an English friend. Summary notices of Job's remarkable experiences have appeared regularly over the past two and a half centuries but have seldom been related to stories of his peers.

The dramatic history, travel, and letters of Ibrahim Abd ar-Rahman, captured as a cavalry officer in Guinea, later a runaway, and then a plantation manager in Natchez, Mississippi, who was freed as an old man and who campaigned to raise money to free his children; whose sense of self and dignity impressed many American leaders, black and white, across the Northern states; and who scared newspaper editors in the Old Southwest before he and his wife gained passage to Liberia, Africa, in 1828, are worthy of a feature movie. Limited versions of his wonderful story have been retold often. Ar-Rahman said he received some education in Timbuktu. The city, as seen in 1828, appears in Fig. 2. For an early depiction of Muslims from Guinea see Fig. 3.

Another strong African and American, Bilali, originally from Guinea but taken to the Bahamas and then to the North American mainland, was a plantation manager supervising 500 to 1,000 slaves—without white overseership. He was also a religious father, an *imam* (Arabic) or *almaamy* (Fulfulde) who in the 1840s began to write a thirteen-page manual in Arabic for his Sapelo Island, Georgia, *umma*—the only known antebellum African Muslim community in the United States. His reticent purchaser, Thomas Spalding—a contributor to some local newspapers—remained mum about his prized slave's accomplishments and acquirements. In the 1930s, however, descendants recalled Bilali and his Muslim daughters for modern interviewers. His "manual"—for years thought to be a diary—still awaits a complete translation.

On the neighboring island of St. Simon's, a comparably competent figure, Salih Bilali, Bilali's friend, had a similarly reticent master. But the latter did write a revealing letter to the most knowledgeable American student of North African languages and culture, William Brown Hodgson—whose name appears often in this book—on his African Muslim's intelligence, leadership skills, and homeland of Mali.

Only fragments of Lamine Kebe's remarks on Africa and his Guinean homeland have been found so far. But his comments on teaching were printed in an American educational journal in 1836—a year after Kebe had returned to Liberia. Kebe and Umar corresponded in Arabic in 1835. The Christian New Yorker who introduced them to one another, Theodore Dwight, Jr., was a professional writer who seems to have sincerely believed that at least some

Fig. 2. View of the City of Timbuktu by Visitor René Caillié, from Caillié, *Travels Through Central Africa to Timbuktu*, 1830.

Fig. 3. Muslim Soldier and Chief in Sangara or Kankan (Guinea), from Alexander Laing, *Travels in the Timanee, Kooranko, and Soolima Countries in Western Africa*, 1825.

Africans were worthy of intellectual respect, but he was also a colonizationist intent on shipping them back to Africa.

Umar ibn Said, captured in a battle between rival armies in Senegal and transported to Charleston, South Carolina, from which he fled to Fayetteville, North Carolina, has also been the subject of several articles over the years. These narratives often create a distance between Umar's life and the legends about him. Umar was a writer, according to several visitors who solicited evidence from him. From at least thirty such mentions, thirteen manuscript pages from the Quran or the Bible, in Arabic, were known to exist before late 1995. Then the manuscript of his sixteen-page "Life," composed in 1831— one of two known autobiographies of slaves written in Arabic in the New World—reappeared. This discovery is significant because only translations by missionaries had been available previously. In these early translations Umar rejects Islam for Christianity—hence the many memorial articles. The original, rediscovered, is being translated now. Preliminary readings, however, suggest that Umar did not deny Islam, but did add Christian prayers to his spiritual stock—a not uncommon practice for religious Muslims among Christians, pleasing to the latter and consistent with the Quran that honors Jesus as an early prophet. Nothing indicates that he started to believe that Jesus was the final prophet or that there were three gods or a three-part God, as Christians suggest in prayers to the Father, the Son, and the Holy Ghost.

Mahommah G. Baquaqua, an indulged child and near-alcoholic adult in Benin—and later in Brazil and Haiti—collaborated with a naive but sympathetic British-born editor on an entertaining sixty-five-page biography-autobiography (Detroit, Michigan,1854) that includes the only known narrative by a one-time slave in Brazil and by an African in an antebellum American college (Central in upstate New York) that had black professors. This source remained completely untapped by historians until the 1970s. Fig. 4 shows three Muslims from areas familiar to Baquaqua before he was taken away.

Mohammed Ali ben Said, who was kidnapped in northern Nigeria and marched across the Sahara Desert, eventually made his way to the United States by way of Russia and Europe. Apparently a quick learner with at least eight languages at his command, Said became a schoolteacher in Detroit around 1860. He wrote, in English, the only known autobiography of an African-born soldier in the Union Army. His Odyssean tale was published in the *Atlantic Monthly* in 1867. That fact did not help him to become better known; the article and he remained out of sight until the 1980s.

About seventy-five other African Muslims who were in America at the same

Fig. 4. Three Muslims in Ghana, from J. Dupuis, *Journal of a Residence in Ashanti*, 1824.

time are introduced in Chapter 2. Much less has been discovered about these potentially interesting stories and instructive informants on unfamiliar peoples, conditions, religions, and cultures. Perhaps they did not meet responsive and trustworthy interviewers with access to presses; perhaps they did not find sufficient encouragement or sufficient reasons to tell their tales. European, American, and Christian interviewers, amanuenses, editors, translators, printers, and observers were impressed with the evident pride, dignity, and intelligence of these people, but during an age when little respect was given to Africans or Muslims, they were usually timid about advertising such reactions, as was the case with those mentioned earlier except within circumscribed areas or according to certain agendas. Job was treated well by humane Englishmen; Abd ar-Rahman was part of a campaign aimed at sending intelligent, self-respecting African Americans away from America, and, perhaps, at stirring Southern guilt and Northern senses of superiority over the matter of slavery. Umar was promoted as a convert to Christianity. The others were made known to a few friends and ethnological specialists. None was taken up by an American abolitionist.

It is undoubtedly true that those Africans who did talk were not in full control over what whites printed. But it is also true that many of these narrators were aware of the agendas of their listeners, and some expressed their own purposes and managed to fulfill them to varying extents. Several of these people left their marks on descendants in the lower Mississippi River valley, in Georgia, and who knows where else? Scholars have only recently begun to investigate possible connections between these early Muslims and Muslim movements that rose in the 1920s in the American North.

Still, together and apart, these eight long stories and shorter glimpses of African Muslims in antebellum America provide valuable contributions to a truly comprehensive story of Americans and tell more about first-generation African Americans than any other single source. These narratives often include

Fig. 5. A Muslim of Kong (now Ivory Coast) in a Military Costume, from Dupuis, *Journal*, 1824.

unique first-person accounts of West African communities, religions, cultures, and troubles at a time when few white people were allowed by African rulers to venture inland from coastal ports or riverbanks. Only three of the narrators had seen whites before they arrived at debarkation points on the coast or on African rivers. None were captured by Europeans or Americans. None were Moors or Arabs; all were Africans from below the Sahara Desert who had been captured in wars or in kidnappings by non-Muslim or Muslim enemies.

Map 1 shows the locations of their homelands in the area Arabs called the *bilad as-Sudan*, or land of the blacks. All of their stories began 200 to 800 miles from any coast. They also began where Islam was strong, in *Dar al-Islam*, where believers were in political control, or where they were gaining strength or comfort or security in *Dar al-kufr*, lands of struggle with unbelievers. Their families were prominent politically, religiously, professionally, commercially, or militarily. Job was in training to be a local *imam*, or religious leader; Bilali probably was too. Abd ar-Rahman was a cavalry officer; Umar was a teacher and trader; Kebe was a schoolteacher. Others were in training for such offices. Job, Abd ar-Rahman, and Kebe had begun their own families in Africa.

They were trained so well in the tenets of their faith that nearly all adhered to the religion of their parents despite years of blandishments by Christian missionaries in the New World. Nearly all wished to return to Africa, despite witnessing the wonders of the Western world and despite what must have been traumatic experiences in the Old. The majority of those discussed in this book had impressive models back home and did not—as some latter-day theorists have presumed—feel the need to adopt white role models.

It may be argued that these people were elite Africans. It is true that they were not from peasant, laboring classes, although some were herders, rice planters, and blacksmiths. It may also be argued that they enjoyed a more established religion, culture, and sense of self than did non-Muslims. But other West African individuals who got caught up in the Atlantic slave trade—Akan, Ashanti, Bambaras, Dahomeans, Ibos, Wolofs, and Yorubas, for notable examples—were equally impressive on this side of the Middle or Bitter Passage, over the "bitter water," as Lamine Kebe called the ocean. Nothing written here should be construed as saying that African Muslims were innately superior to fellow Africans who were not Muslims.

Strong practitioners of indigenous religions appear to have been no more likely than Muslims or those who mixed the two to become "Sambos"—psychologically dulled, culturally deprived creatures, according to one modern theory—because of the trauma of capture, of being torn out of Africa, and of being thrown into the foul slave ships plying the Bitter Passage to the New World. In fact, several Muslims, non-Muslims, and non-Christians earned names such as King, Prince, Queen, or Cleopatra by the proud but politic ways in which they carried themselves. The strongest people found ways to balance accommodations they made to their purchasers against accommodations they wrested from the latter. The stories of non-Muslim individuals brought to the New World also deserve attention; here, however, the focus is on African Muslims, who have been peculiarly slighted in American history and literature.

Perhaps I ought to add that all of the leading figures in this book are men. These stories were gathered by men in an era when women were only beginning to be writers who could follow their own agendas. Still, we do hear something about Job's wives; about Isabella, obstetric practitioner and gynecologist and Baptist wife of Abd ar-Rahman; about female teachers in Africa known by Kebe; about the wives and daughters of Bilali Muhammad and his friend Salih Bilali and female descendants of both in the 1930s; and about some abused and some angelic women known to Mahommah Baquaqua.

Considered together, the stories collected here also involve—not always in a positive light—prominent American figures: statesmen, ethnologists, colonizationists, novelists, historians, and racial propagandists of several sorts. These include James Oglethorpe, founder of the colony of Georgia, who helped Job escape American slavery; President John Quincy Adams, whom Abd ar-Rahman called the best piece of furniture in the White House; Mark Twain, whose irrepressible racism led him to imagine a cannibal in a portrait of Abd ar-Rahman; and the still-popular historical novelist James A. Michener, who thought that novelist Alex Haley erred when he made his ancestral African hero of *Roots* (1976) a Muslim. Michener declared that Haley had not given a "true reflection of the past," and no American or European historians disagreed.

That a "true reflection of the past" including African Muslims had to wait until the nation's bicentennial, when Haley transformed himself into a latter-day *griot* or *jelli* (West African family praise-singers and historians), is due to several causes that will be explored later. Suffice it to say that the oldest is the ancient struggle between Christianity and Islam that began in the seventh century of the Common Era (CE), when the advent of the latter led to spiritual, intellectual, economic, and military conflict and enslavement by each of the other's followers into the nineteenth century. From Columbus's day through the thirteen colonies' declaration of independence on July 4, 1776, and into the early days of U.S. history, the struggle against Muslims was one of the most significant issues in Christendom. Muslims occasionally appeared in political and literary works by Europeans and sometimes in those by Americans. The first treaty of the new nation was made with Morocco; one of its first international military adventures, on "the shores of Tripoli," North Africa, is memorialized in "The Marine's Hymn"; and a number of stories were told of Christians—especially women— enslaved by Muslims around the Mediterranean. The most trustworthy novel on the latter subject was Royall Tyler's *The Algerine Captive* (1797).

African Muslim individuals, however, were largely unnoticed. In the nineteenth century Europeans gained industrial and technological superiority over Muslims, making the latter as unthreatening as other Africans. The most influential European philosophers, David Hume (1746), Immanuel Kant (1764), and G.W.F. Hegel (1813) declared—admittedly without sufficient evidence— that Africans had not and could not become self-governing, rational, spiritual, or literate and, according to Hegel, could only approach "civilization" with Muslim or Christian help. American philosophers such as Thomas Jefferson (1785) and Noah Webster (1843) overlooked any examples (Job, poet Phillis Wheatley, autobiographer Olaudah Equiano, and others) that suggested a different perspective, though Job was noticed as a Moorish African.

Trends in the treatment of African Muslims in our national story have been closely related to the treatment of Africans and African Americans in our lives and literature, of course. Abd ar-Rahman gained some fame in 1828, as did Umar in the 1840s and 1850s. Novelist William A. Caruthers included short recognitions of African Muslims in his work in the 1830s; single novel writer David Brown included one in his book in 1850. In the 1850s there was a sudden burst of writing—essays, biographies, histories, poetry, and novels—by African Americans and some European American allies and enemies. Not long thereafter, however, the enemies prevailed, and nearly everything in print about Africans became condescending or negative. A few African Muslim individuals were noticed shortly around our Civil War, before a kind of suppression of information about such people that lasted into the 1980s. But in his controversial novella "Benito Cereno" (1856), Herman Melville did not clearly admit that his major African characters, literate and rebellious slaves, were Muslims, despite calling attention to his historical source, which did recognize that they were believers in Allah. Harriet Beecher Stowe's titular hero of her novel *Dred, A Tale of the Great Dismal Swamp* (1856) was the son of Mandingoes—usually Muslim in her time—but she did not suggest any such religious heritage.

One effect of such propaganda and suppression was an early disidentification between antebellum African Americans and Muslims. For example, leading black abolitionists Henry Highland Garnet and Martin R. Delany prided themselves on having Mandingo grandparents, but neither publicly expressed any Muslim influence. This misapprehension lasted until the 1920s and the rise of the Nation of Islam, although there were some African Americans who maintained that they were not wholly or only African or black. Several small populations, Free Moors of the Carolinas, Malungeons in Tennessee, Delaware Moors, and Virginia Maroons, have insisted upon Muslim beginnings from colonial times.

After the Civil War, three prominent Southern writers did recognize, in their fashions, African Muslims in America. In 1867, Mark Twain saw a portrait of a "dignified old darkey" in Hartford, Connecticut, and was told the story of the subject, Abd ar-Rahman. As was his usual way, Twain began a reasonable retelling of the black person's story but could not refrain from marring it at the end by declaring that he hoped the old man was happily back in Africa eating "niggers he could not sell." Twain's friend George Washington Cable wrote several times of the presence of what he was pleased to call "Arab-Africans" in Louisiana. He and another of Twain's friends, Joel Chandler Harris, creator of the black Uncle Remus who told stories about Brer Rabbit to a white boy but not to a black, shared the notion that some slaves were superior to the majority because they were Arabs and not Africans. Harris perversely, it seems, based an African-despising, enslaved Arab Muslim character he called Aaron on the historical Bilali, who despised Christians, not Africans.

For a long time thereafter, no African Muslims appeared in American texts or novels, although there were some local newspaper recollections of Umar, the "convert" to Christianity, and a translation of his "Life" did get published in 1925. But Africans generally were still treated as if they were uncivilizable until the 1950s. White accounts of Africa told about European and American heroes attempting to save Africans from themselves; Muslims in Africa were reportedly only slightly more enlightened but were still taking slaves long after Europeans had stopped. Seldom did anything respectable come out of any Africans. Indeed, late in this period, a very popular novel (Kyle Onstott's *Mandingo*, 1957) was preceded by an erroneous but authoritatively presented one-page assertion that Mandingoes were Muslims but "distinctly not Negroes."

Finally, however, in the 1950s, serious histories and studies of Africans, African Americans, and Muslims began to appear. Scholars were responding, at first timidly, to a three-part assault on European religious, social, political, and philosophical presumptions in the decade when, starting with Ghana in 1957, Africans were beginning to regain their independence after some eighty years of European rule; in the same year the Montgomery, Alabama, civil rights movement was joined by Martin Luther King, Jr., and African Americans were beginning to gain constitutional rights that European Americans had long enjoyed. Meanwhile Muslim people were beginning to rise again in Egypt and elsewhere after a century of decreasing power—except in Africa where numbers were increasing.

The first study of Islam in West Africa—where more than half of all North American slaves came from—appeared in 1959. Still, Muslims in Africa inspired no more than a sentence in any history of America or slavery until 1968. Even then a book on Job, Douglas Grant's *Fortunate Slave,* and another on Job and nine other Africans caught up in the Atlantic slave trade, *Africa Remembered*, edited by Philip D. Curtin and others, emphasized the African aspects of their narratives. A mint-julep-and-magnolia-scented third book, James Register's *Jallon: Arabic Prince of Old Natchez,* followed earlier leads and de-Africanized Abd ar-Rahman. A year after Haley's *Roots,* in 1977, Terry Alford published an admirably researched and beautifully told biography of Abd ar-Rahman—but the title, *Prince Among Slaves,* sets his hero, who married a black and Baptist woman, above other African Americans. In that same year, Toni Morrison was curiously coy as she borrowed Muslim names (Solomon, Balaly, Medina, Omar, Ryna, and Muhammet) and stories about flying Africans from the Georgia Writers Project's *Drums and Shadows* without acknowledging their religious provenance that brought a Muslim spin to her novel *Song of Solomon.*

My 1984 book, *African Muslims in Antebellum America: A Sourcebook*, was the first to bring all the then available stories and references together. Since then, a cameo appearance by a Muslim elder in a movie, Julie Dash's *Daughters of the Dust* (1992); a full-length philosophical-linguistic study of contexts for the writings of Job, Bilali, Kebe, and Umar by Ronald A. T. Judy in 1993; relevant articles by B. G. Martin, Muhammad al-Ahari, and Michael A. Gomez and part of a chapter by William S. McFeely in 1994; and some reprints of shorter biographical pieces have brought these stories forward again. But the same few names are always raised. Too many others are still being forgotten.

Before elaborating further on these issues, listen to some hints of what has been omitted from our national story and understanding of Africa and Africans. Nine of our narrators, including Lamine Kebe, express themselves carefully and boldly.

I was desired by [Job], . . . to draw up an Account of him agreeable to the Information he had given me at different Times, and to the Truth of the Facts, which I had either been a Witness to, or [was] personally concerned in upon his Account.

—Thomas Bluett, English friend of Job Ben Solomon, London, 1734

I will answer for every Negro of the true faith [Islam] but not for these Christian dogs of yours.

—Bilali Muhammad to his master, as he prepared defenses against a possible British raid on Sapelo Island, Georgia, 1815

He will not allow that the Americans are as polite and hospitable a people as the Moors [Muslims]—nor that they enjoy a tenth part of the comfort they do—and that for learning and talents [Americans] are far behind them.

—From a Quaker merchant's diary on an unnamed, literate "Moorish" slave met on the Mississippi River, 1822

I tell you, the Testament very good law; you no follow it; you [Mississippians] no pray often enough; you greedy after money. . . . See, you want more land, more neegurs; you make neegur work hard, make more cotton. Where you find dat in your law?

—Ibrahim Abd ar-Rahman, Natchez, Mississippi, 1828

When I came to the Christian country, my religion was the religion of "Mohammed, the Apostle of God—may God have mercy upon him and give him peace.". . . And now I pray "Our Father, etc.," in the words of Jesus the Messiah.

—from a translation of the autobiography in Arabic by Umar ibn Said, Fayetteville, North Carolina, 1831

There are good men in America, but all are very ignorant of Africa. Write down what I tell you exactly as I say it, and be careful to distinguish between what I have seen and what I have only heard other people speak of. They may have made some mistakes; but if you put down exactly what I say, by and by, when good men go to Africa, they will say, Paul told the truth.

—"Old Paul," or Lamine Kebe, New York City, 1835

I had never seen white people before; and they appeared to me the ugliest creatures in the world.

> —from "the man who prayed five times a day,"
> in Charles Ball's slave narrative, Pittsburgh, 1854

The [drunken, abusive sailor] sat down and ate like a christian, but this was not till I had let him see a little of my own ugliness, and had threatened to beat him.

> —from Mahommah Baquaqua's *Biography,* Detroit, 1854

I cannot help thinking that the way I was baptized was not right, for I think that I ought to have known perfectly well the nature of the thing beforehand.

> —Nicholas Said, on a Russian experience, Boston, 1867

There is not much comfort here for those who would presume that all Africans who might be induced to reveal their feelings would sound defeated or detached and ashamed of their homelands or people or culture and eager to please American saviors. On the contrary, these are proud and critical voices, emanating from possessors of extraordinarily strong identities and an obviously powerful faith. Here they speak for many individuals once thought to be lost forever: many thousands who were carried from Africa to America and reduced to slavery but not silence in the era of the international slave trade.

Each of these speakers is discussed further in later chapters. As noted above, six appear in chapters devoted exclusively to their stories; two share a chapter, and almost seventy-five others—about whom less information has been found—are brought together in Chapter 2. The following pages also comprise five maps; eight portraits of seven African Muslims who came to America (and four portraits of descendants who in the late 1930s recalled Muslim parents and grandparents); eighteen documents in Arabic that were composed in America plus translations or references to fourteen more; and biographies, autobiographies, and notes of various lengths and purposes on the other African Muslims who were caught up in the Atlantic slave trade between 1730 and 1860. This introductory chapter concludes with relevant, highly compressed background material.

Centuries of Christian-Muslim confrontations, condescensions, presumptions, prejudices, misrepresentations, and mistreatment made Kebe's conclusion about Western ignorance of Africa inevitable for his own time and ours. Less than a century after 622 CE, the traditional date of the founding of Islam in Arabia by the Prophet Muhammad, previously Christian Egypt and North Africa had become Muslim territory. Shortly thereafter, Christian Spain and Palestine and Eastern Europe were conquered by Muslims. Christians considered Muhammad an upstart schismatic who was dividing their spiritual and political world order—such as it was after the slow fall of Rome between 453 and 600 CE—into three religions celebrating one God as found in early Jewish writings, their own New Testament, and the Quran. Muslims, those who followed Islam ("submission" to God or Allah—a compassionate but just creator), understood the message in the Quran as a recitation from God to Muhammad that built upon and corrected the messages of the respected Jewish prophets: Adam, Noah, Moses, and Abraham as well as the Christians' Jesus. Muhammad, believed by Muslims to be the last of the creator's prophets, recited Allah's words to his creatures on the latter's obligations to believe in the one God—unlike Christians, who prayed not only to God but also to a son and mother of God—to pray publicly, to give alms to the poor, to fast and follow dietary codes, to dress modestly, to become one with the community of believers, and to exert themselves on behalf of the principles of this faith.

Some sharing and a lot of competition between Christians and Muslims on several levels led to confrontational military struggles, particularly the Crusades against Muslims in Palestine and Muslim counterattacks in the eleventh, twelfth, and thirteenth centuries. When the Crusades were halted around a few captured cities in the Holy Land, Europeans attempted to sail around Africa and Muslim lands in order to get to the riches of Asia. These ventures eventually led to the "discovery" of America in 1492; a continuing enslavement by Christians and Muslims of each other whenever possible; and the adoption and refinement of ways to grow Asian and African crops such as sugar, rice, indigo, and cotton that Europeans wanted but did not grow in their own countries. African knowledge and experience and labor were needed; Europeans tried Native American labor, but those people died from unfamiliar diseases and harsh treatment. Africans had been exposed to many European diseases and could do nothing about their treatment in America, so their expertise turned into labor for themselves and profit for their masters.

But these are long and complex side issues. My present focus is more limited. The story of Islam's spread below the Sahara Desert, from about 1100 CE, by Berbers from the north and Arabs from the east into the *bilad as-Sudan*—the land of the blacks—has recently inspired a number of books. This spread was mostly peaceful and was propagated by way of Muslim visitors with appealing spiritual, political, military, medical, technical, and commercial powers. Sometimes local rulers took on Muslim advisers; some studied, then adopted, Muslim ways and imposed them on their courts or people; sometimes Muslim visitors settled down and intermarried as they provided services or became local representatives of distant trading networks. Others started Quranic schools for children of Muslims and interested non-Muslims.

Attempts to impose the new religion led to various responses, of course. Formerly Christian people or those practicing indigenous religions and their leaders across North Africa sometimes joined in or gave in and adjusted; others—Berbers and Tuaregs—incorporated some elements and rejected others. On the side of the Sahara Desert, other people further south, such as the Wolofs of Senegal and the Bambaras of Mali, rejected Islam until late in the nineteenth century; and the Mossi of Burkina Faso have done so into our own time. In much of West Africa Islam has been modified according to indigenous needs, as it has been by other peoples in its spread to the Pacific Ocean, and as West Africans and others have modified Christianity. There have been and continue to be significant military, political, cultural, and spiritual struggles and accommodations between Muslims and Saharan and sub-Saharan people not influenced by Christians. This has been a long and complicated history; some parts of it will be told as they relate to individuals discussed in this book.

Another reason for so long and complicated a history has to do with racial attitudes. Muslim Arabs—like Christians—brought their prejudices with them. Both presumed that indigenous African religions and the people who protected them were not worthy of respect or tolerance. Both brought scriptural support for enslaving the latter. And many of both presumed that black people—so unlike themselves—might make better workers in hot climes than themselves. In the Quran Allah praises all the colors of people he has created—so color difference was not supposed to lead to a total dehumanization, though it often led to enslavement. The Quran offers rules and humane advice on the treatment of non-Muslims and slaves. These rules include teaching the religion to slaves and the children of slaves, treating slaves as valuable dependents by not overworking or underfeeding them, and adopting and freeing the children of slave mothers. Muhammad and other leaders set the example by freeing slaves who joined the religion. The Prophet's first convert, after his wife, was the Ethiopian Bilali, whom he freed and honored further by appointing him as the first *muezzin*, or summoner to prayer. This tale explains the ing him as the first *muezzin*, or summoner to prayer. This tale explains the popularity of the name Bilali in West Africa; four people in the following stories enjoyed it.

Arab Muslims and African converts were, however, members of nonpeasant, trading, teaching, and traveling classes living among Muslim, non-Muslim—or, indeed, anti-Muslim—people with whom they farmed, herded, traded, fought, and intermarried. The willingness of Muslims to intermarry with local people and to live like them contrasted favorably with the attitudes of Christian missionaries. The children of such Muslims soon became African and black as well as Muslim. Much of their lives and cultures were shared with their neighbors, who had their own religions, cultures, and politics, which powerfully influenced regional and local Islamic practices. Muslim treatment of slaves in West Africa during the slave trade era also seems to have been more respectful of West African practices and religious teachings than that of Christians. Ideally, wherever Muslims gained power, they offered freedom to nonbelievers who accepted Islam. Those people of the book (Christians and Jews) who paid a tax, or *jizya*, were allowed to practice their own religions unmolested. In practice, however, some Muslims were no better than other religious or ethnic groups in their obedience to the higher dictates. The taking of slaves and marching them off to distant lands was brutal whenever and wherever and by whomever it happened. Several narrators of tales in this book describe how they fell into captivity. Muslims were both captors of and liable to be captives of non-Muslim rivals at various times. Sometimes Muslims were taken prisoner and sold by rival Muslims who disagreed with their captives' principles and practices.

As European travelers in Africa noted, Mandingo and Fulbe people were prominent in the slave trade, as they were in all trade. But they were not all slavers, and they had their codes for the business, as we shall see. Nor may these two Muslim peoples be singled out in any simplistic way as is common in histories of Africa. Non-Muslim peoples such as the Bambaras, Ashanti, Dahomeans, Yorubans, and Ibos also captured and sold thousands of Africans who were sent to the New World. Each of these peoples was ethnocentric, and all had leaders who were sure that their accomplishments naturally set them above others. These attitudes of Muslim and non-Muslim slave traders were similar to those of European and American slave-takers—surely one reason why native slavers were publicized by the latter as peculiarly admirable Africans, although they were undoubtedly dangerous competitors.

At least thirteen of the individuals discussed in this book came from the more prominent peoples involved in the spread of Islam in West Africa above the Gulf of Guinea: Ten were Fulbe or Tukolor, two were Mande or Mandingo, and Lamine Kebe was a Serahule or Soninke schoolteacher. Others were in training to be *qadi*s (lawyers) or *imam*s (religious-political leaders—Islam does not differentiate between the two). Three were military officers; another was a prominent trader. Several were students. The majority were from large towns where local practice regularly divided the community into sections based on ethnicity and religion. From 1725 to the middle of the nineteenth century, military *jihads* were led by Fulbe against economic, political, and religious enemies in Futa Jallon, Futa Toro, Massina, and what is now northern Nigeria. At least three of the Fulbe considered here were caught up in wars with Muslims who were somehow disagreeable to other Muslims. Others were involved in struggles against or allied with non-Muslim powers which led to their transportation to the New World. Anti-Muslim Mande, Bambaras, Ashanti, Dahomeans, and Yorubans made some of the captures in war or in kidnappings described in these stories.

Much, then, can be learned about Muslim political training, long-distance trade, internal troubles, and religious preparation and literacy wherever our narrators went. The Tukolor, a sedentary, darker branch of the Fulbe whose origins are still debated (who also included the nomadic, lighter, "red" Fulbe who were slow to become Muslim), thought other Muslims were less devout. Perhaps this notion was true because the Tukolor proved to be the most likely to adhere to Islam in the New World. The Fulbe were also the most proud, as on both continents they announced their superiority to all non-Fulbe, whether black or white. This air of superiority was often marked by white Americans, who conveniently presumed that it applied only to other black people.

Those who traded over long routes learned a lot about other peoples and their geography. A freeman from Jamaica, Abu Bakr as-Siddik, supplied a long list of African place names and related them to one another geographically in 1836. He referred to sites in an area larger than the portion of the United States between the Mississippi River and the Atlantic Ocean. Several of these narrators learned more about West Africa when they were marched from home, or wherever they were captured, to distant coasts. Clearly, a number of those in this book—had they been encouraged and seen any value to themselves in doing so—could have been very informative about what was called for far too long an unknown continent filled with ignorant people.

The geographical origins shown in Map 1 place some of these people in *Dar al-Islam,* among believers who had been Muslims in Senegal, Timbuktu, or near Lake Chad since 1100 CE; or among those in southern Mali, the Gambia, and Guinea who had become Muslims in the era of both peaceful and military expansion from 1725 into the middle of the nineteenth century; or among the *kufr* (unbelievers) in Burkina Faso, the Ivory Coast, and Benin.

None of the Africans described herein were taken by white men, who, through most of the period from 1700 to 1860, were restricted by West African rulers to tiny footholds on the coast or along riverbanks. Only three had seen white men before they arrived at the baracoons, or holding pens, where prisoners awaited slave ships. Two of them presumed that they might be eaten by these strangers. Africans often told Europeans tales of cannibals just beyond the boundaries within which they restricted whites and the European goods they wanted to monopolize. Apparently, they also told such tales about European slavers. Some Muslim rulers complained that European, and later American, slavers wanted only people rather than gold, gum, ivory, skins, palm oil, wood, or other trade products. However, none of these rulers, or non-Muslim rulers for that matter, wanted to give up to other Africans the European products they imported and traded inland in exchange for slaves.

Most European and American reports on West Africa emphasized conflicts rather than cooperation between Muslims and non-Muslims. Some Muslims, including the Fulbe—known as slave catchers and traders—were at times peaceable and alternately strange and useful neighbors who traded, translated, transcribed, advised, and accommodated themselves to varying degrees to indigenous and Christian people. It is not yet possible to tell how many Muslims were in West Africa or were taken out of it in the era of the international slave trade. In my previous book, taking into consideration available figures related to Africans sent from ports serving hinterland areas from which Muslims might have been taken, figures on arrivals from the Senegambia—the source for the most sought-after slaves, especially by American slavers working fast between the end of the Revolutionary War and January 1, 1808, when the trade was supposed to be legally ended—and relevant details from the stories herein, I boldly estimated that between 5 and 10 percent of all slaves from ports between Senegal and the Bight of Benin, from which half of all Africans were sent to North America, were Muslims. If the total number of arrivals was eleven million, as scholars have concluded, then there may have been about forty thousand African Muslims in the colonial and pre–Civil War territory making up the United States before 1860. In the near future, the systematic gathering of records on slave trading ports on both sides of the Atlantic Ocean and studies by David Eltis, David Richardson, and others of the trade as it touched on several British, French, Dutch, Spanish, and American cities and towns will lead to better figures and descriptions.

Today, Muslims are the majority in Senegal, the Gambia, Guinea, Mali, and Niger; number more than twenty million in Nigeria; and are respectably represented in Sierra Leone, Liberia, the Ivory Coast, Burkina Faso, Ghana, and Benin. In the United States, Muslims amount to some six or seven million, a number equal to the number of any single Christian denomination in the country. A third of these may be African and African American. They and their role in our history and their relations with and effect on Islam elsewhere cannot be neglected any longer.

Finally, a few words about the literacy of these people. The Fulbe were proud of their Quranic schools and their ability to read and write for the greater glory of God—and of the Fulbe, perhaps. Their literacy included writing Arabic and their own language using the phonetic Arabic letters. At least six of the Fulbe mentioned in this book wrote in Arabic in America—and they usually wrote what they chose to write: assertions of their faith in the words of Allah. Job, who authorized a friend to write his *Memoirs* in English, was supposed to have written a letter to his father from Maryland in 1733, in Arabic, of course. Unfortunately, this significant manuscript has not yet been found. There are copies of letters in Arabic from Job to English friends, written from Africa, that do not agree with what Job dictated to his secretaries as translations. In the Arabic, he appears to be praising Allah for his good fortune; in the English, he praises an earthly benefactor. He may have known how to write only religious, and perhaps commercial formulae—as he was a trader—or he may not have seen the necessity to write more elaborately for people who knew no Arabic. Probably he could read better than he could write; when he was in London, he helped some Englishmen translate Arabic writings.

Ar-Rahman also wrote a letter to his father in Arabic that was sent to Morocco by the U.S. government. Later he wrote variations on the first chapter of the Quran (the Fatiha, or Opening) for a number of people he met in the Northeast. This limited range of writing suggests a limited literacy, but again, it may have been clear that he had no readers of Arabic and thus need not bother. That a Rev. John F. Shroeder was pleased by ar-Rahman's writing Arabic "with correctness and fluency, . . . neatness and rapidity"—after thirty years of being out of Africa—could mean that he was better educated than extant manuscripts suggest. But it could also mean that he could do more in the presence of a reader of Arabic. Shroeder said that ar-Rahman "has read and written for me a great deal of Arabic." Unfortunately, these manuscripts have not been found either.

Bilali's single known literary effort has survived. Clearly he struggled, as he seems to have made three or four tries to write rules for his Muslim community in Georgia. His work, discussed in Chapter 5, is incomplete and difficult to decipher. Umar ibn Said, however, wrote often, and fourteen of his manuscripts are extant; thirteen others are referred to or are quoted from by interested parties. A beautifully written two-page—and there may have been more—manuscript includes a large design enclosing some words, part of a long chapter from the Quran, and some pieces most likely from commentators on the Quran. Umar wrote an informative sixteen-page autobiography preceded by part of the chapter of the Quran also found in the earlier manuscript, three Lord's Prayers, two Twenty-third Psalms, two lists of his master's family names, a kind of commentary on Christian prayers, and parts of three short chapters of the Quran. Most of these followed traditional invocations to Allah and Muhammad. Charno or Chierno supplied our frontispiece, the first Surah or chapter of the Quran, for a nosy traveler. It is likely, from his proud attitude, that the "Moor on the Mississippi" was also a Fulbe. He also wrote the Fatiha for a wandering white man.

As a Mandingo slave in Jamaica, Abu Bakr as-Siddiq, who kept plantation records in English using Arabic letters, also wrote a heartfelt autobiography in Arabic. A second Mandingo in Jamaica, known only by his Christian name "William Rainsford," wrote excerpts from the Quran. Another, "Charles Larten," was said to have written out a complete Quran from memory. Yet another, Mohammed Kaba, corresponded with Abu Bakr about the faith.

A Mandingo in South Carolina, slave of a Captain Anderson, also wrote passages from the Quran. Another Mandingo, London, attempted an exercise that—had we more than the five lines provided by a quite respectable translator—must be a linguistic treasure, as he transcribed in Arabic letters the Gospel of John and some hymns in the black English he heard in Georgia. Perhaps he was a convert, or perhaps he saw nothing absolutely anti-Muslim in what he was transcribing.

Some Muslims could read and not write. Salih Bilali was one. Mahommah Baquaqua from Benin forgot nearly all of his Arabic. He had not liked school; there is, however an "Allah" written in Arabic on one of Baquaqua's seven surviving letters written in English. Nicholas Said said he had learned to read Arabic and was learning Turkish when he was kidnapped. Obviously they, and several non-Fulbe and non-Mandingo peers such as Kebe, a Serahule, had not forgotten the Quranic school lessons they had learned in Africa. Umar and ar-Rahman wrote Arabic after being away from it for thirty years or more. Writing, to a Muslim, is believing and worshipping. These men undoubtedly found solace and guidance in their memories of Allah's words as recorded by the Prophet in the Quran, and in the traditions they had brought with them. Writing had set them apart as commercially and spiritually useful magical men at home. It gave them some standing in the New World, particularly among those who decided that the literate slaves must be Moors or Arabs because they would not credit such a possibility as literacy in an African. One wonders how these Muslims must have felt when they were among illiterate slaveholders, or among white Americans who strove desperately to de-Africanize them.

Chapter 2 introduces the remaining African Muslims about whom less has been found, including two of those quoted above. Following introductions to each of them, I draw some generalizations about African Muslims in antebellum America. As more students look into relevant records, these people will undoubtedly become less exotic.

SELECTED READINGS
African Muslims in America

Morroe Berger, the first historian to attempt to relate America's early and late African Muslims, has concluded that the American black Muslims of today owe little to black Muslim predecessors such as those mentioned in this text; see "The Black Muslims," *Horizon* 6 (Winter 1964), 53–54, n. 5. See also Clyde-Ahmad Winters, "Roots and Islam in Slave America," *Al-Ittihad* (October–November 1976), 19. But several scholars, including Aminah McCloud at Depaul University, Muhammad al-Ahari in Chicago, and Prince-A-Cuba (E. D. Beynon and Prince-A-Cuba, "Master Fard Muhammad: Detroit History," [1938] [reprinted Newport News, Va.: United Brothers & United Sisters Communications Systems, 1990]), are finding evidence on the rise of the Nation of Islam and other American Muslim movements that challenges that presumption.

For examples of antebellum Muslim manifestations recalled almost a century later, see chapters on Sapelo and St. Simon's islands in Savannah Unit of the Georgia Writers Project of the Works Projects Administration, *Drums and Shadows: Survival Studies Among the Georgia Coastal Negroes* (1940) (reprinted Athens: University of Georgia, 1986).

More information on these Georgia Muslims and others may be found in Allan D. Austin, *African Muslims in Antebellum America: A Sourcebook* (New York: Garland, 1984); and "Islamic Identities in Africans in North America in the Days of Slavery, 1731–1865," *Islam et Societes au Sud du Sahara* 7 (November 1993), 205–219.

A work that needs to be revisited is Alex Haley, *Roots* (Garden City, N.Y.: Doubleday, 1976); compare James A. Michener, "Roots, Unique in Its Time," *New York Times Book Review*, February 26, 1977, 41.

See also the following works

Robert J. Allison, *The Crescent Obscured: The United States and the Muslim World, 1776–1815* (New York: Oxford University Press, 1995).

Michael A. Gomez, "Muslims in Early America," *Journal of Southern History* 60 (November 1994), 671–709.

Yvonne Haddad, "A Century of Islam in America," *The Muslim World Today: Occasional Paper no. 4*, Washington, D. C.: Middle East Institute, 1986.

Gwendolyn Midlo Hall, *Africans in Colonial Louisiana: The Development of Afro-Creole Culture in the 18th Century* (Baton Rouge: Louisiana State University Press, 1992).

Ronald T. Judy, *(Dis)Forming the American Canon: African-Arabic Slave Narratives and the Vernacular* (Minneapolis: University of Minnesota Press, 1993).

Michael A. Köszegi and J. Gordon Melton, eds., *Islam in North America: A Sourcebook.* (New York: Garland, 1993).

William S. McFeely, *Sapelo's People: A Long Walk to Freedom* (New York: Norton, 1994).

On the African Slave Trade

George E. Brooks, Jr., *Yankee Traders, Old Coasters, and African Middlemen* (Boston: Boston University Press, 1970).

Philip D. Curtin, ed., *Africa Remembered: Narratives by West Africans from the Era of the Slave Trade* (Madison: University of Wisconsin Press, 1967).

Philip D. Curtin, *The Atlantic Slave Trade: A Census* (Madison: University of Wisconsin Press, 1964).

Basil Davidson, *Black Mother: The Years of the African Slave Trade* (Boston: Little, Brown, 1961).

James A. Rawley, *The Transatlantic Slave Trade: A History* (New York: Norton, 1981).

Walter Rodney, "Upper Guinea and the Significance of the Origins of Africans Enslaved in the New World," *Journal of Negro History*, 4 (October 1969), 327–345.

Slavery in Africa

David Brion Davis's otherwise impressive *Problem of Slavery in Western Culture* (Ithaca, N.Y.: Cornell University Press, 1966) fails to impress in areas relevant to this collection. Davis opined, "Moslems . . . were inclined to think of black Africans as a race who were born to be slaves" (citing only the *Encyclopedia of Islam* and Edwin William Lane's translation of the *Arabian Nights*). Davis apparently sees no "problem of slavery" in Muslim culture. This will not do as an explanation of the variety of Islamic societies in Africa, nor of the advances Islam has made in Africa largely because of the efforts of black proselytizers such as the Serahules. He does add a footnote about Job Ben Solomon, who he says was patronized by the English and "offered no criticism of the slave system" (pp. 50, 479, n. 78). Davis knows no one was criticizing slavery as a system in 1734. His discussions of Islam and slavery leap from the thirteenth century to the late nineteenth in *Slavery and Human Progress* (New York: Oxford University Press, 1984).

Frederick Cooper, *Plantation Slavery on the East Coast of Africa* (New Haven: Yale University Press, 1977).

Basil Davidson, "Slaves or Captives? Some Notes on Fantasy and Fact," in Nathan I. Huggins et al., eds., *Key Issues in the Afro-American Experience*, vol. 1 (New York: Harcourt, 1971).

Joseph E. Inikori and Stanley L. Engerman, eds., *The Atlantic Slave Trade: Effects on Economies, Societies, and Peoples in Africa, the Americas, and Europe* (Durham: Duke University Press, 1992).

Martin A. Klein, "Servitude Among the Wolof and Serers of Senegambia," in Suzanne Miers and Igor Kopytoff, eds., *Slavery in Africa: Historical and Anthropological Perspectives* (Madison: University of Wisconsin Press, 1977).

Paul E. Lovejoy, *Transformations in Slavery: A History of Slavery in Africa* (Cambridge: Cambridge University Press, 1983).

Patrick Manning, *Slavery and African Life: Occidental, Oriental, and African Slave Trades* (New York: Cambridge University Press, 1990).

Barbara L. Solow, ed., *Slavery and the Rise of the Atlantic System* (Cambridge: Cambridge University Press, 1991).

Africa and Islam

Ahmed Ali, trans. *Al-Qur'ān: A Contemporary Translation* (Princeton: Princeton University Press, 1984).

J. F. A. Ajayi and Michael Crowder, eds., *History of West Africa,* 2 vols. (New York: Columbia University Press, 1976, 1974).

Edward W. Blyden, *Christianity, Islam, and the Negro Race* (1888) (reprinted Baltimore: Black Classic Press, 1994).

Peter B. Clarke, *West Africa and Islam: A Study of Religious Development from the18th to the 20th Century* (London: Edward Arnold, 1984).

Frederick Mathewson Denny, *An Introduction to Islam* (New York: Macmillan, 1985).

Mervyn Hiskett, *The Sword of Truth: The Life and Times of the Shehu Usuman Dan Fodio* (New York: Oxford University Press, 1973); and *The Development of Islam in West Africa* (New York: Longman, 1984).

I. M. Lewis, ed., *Islam in Tropical Africa,* 2nd ed. (Bloomington: Indiana University and International African Institute, 1980).

Walter Rodney, *A History of the Upper Guinea Coast: 1545–1800* (London: Oxford University Press, 1970).

Lamin O. Sanneh, *The Jakhanke: The History of an Islamic Clerical People of the Senegambia* (London: International African Institute, 1979).

J. Spencer Trimingham, *Islam in West Africa* (1959) and *A History of Islam in West Africa* (London: Oxford University Press, 1962).

John Ralph Willis, ed. *Slaves and Slavery in Muslim Africa,* vol. I: *Islam and the Ideology of Slavery* (London: Cass, 1985).

————. *Studies in West African Islamic History,* vol. I: *The Cultivators of Islam* (London: Cass, 1979).

African Muslim Literacy and Literature

Birago Diop, *Tales of Amadou Koumba,* trans. Dorothy S. Blair. (London: Oxford University Press, 1966). Senegal Wolof Muslim indigenous folktales.

Jack Goody, "Restricted Literacy in Northern Ghana," and Ivor Wilks, "The Transmission of Islamic Learning in the Western Sudan," in Jack Goody, ed., *Literacy in Traditional Societies* (Cambridge: Cambridge University Press, 1968).

Kenneth W. Harrow, ed., *Faces of Islam in African Literature* (Portsmouth, N.H.: Heinemann, 1991). A wide-ranging, useful look at Islam(s) in West Africa.

Cheikh Hamidou Kane, *Ambiguous Adventure* (1963) (reprinted New York: Collier, 1969). Novel's hero is given early Quranic training by Tukolor Fula teacher.

Camara Laye, *The African Child,* trans. James Kirkup (London: Fontana, 1965). Novel's hero is born into a preliterate Guinean Malinké Muslim world—but is pushed to read the Quran.

Condé Maryse, *Segu* (New York: Viking, 1987). Novel re-creates Malian Muslim-Bambara conflicts in the nineteenth century.

Mildred Mortimer, *Journeys Through the French African Novel* (Portsmouth, N. H.: Heinemann, 1990).

See also Judy, cited earlier.

Fig. 6. Yarrow Mamout of Georgetown, D.C., from Oil Painting by Charles Willson Peale, 1819; courtesy of Historical Society of Pennsylvania.

2

Glimpses of Seventy-Five
African Muslims
in Antebellum North America

This chapter brings together short glimpses—all that is now available—of more than seventy-five African Muslims who were brought to North America in the pre–Civil War period. I will add narratives of and notes on people brought to the islands of the Caribbean and glance at others brought to Spanish and Portuguese America to round out my introduction to this dispersal of Africans. Each adds, of course, to what is known about these early immigrants.

First, a mostly chronological list for those about whom we have dates and information beyond names alone.

When Job Ben Solomon was brought to the British colony of Maryland in 1730 he was accompanied by his translator, Lamine Ndiaye or Jay, who would eventually be returned to Africa. His story makes up a small part of the next chapter. They probably arrived at the same time as Yarrow Mamout. A wonderful oil portrait was painted in 1819 by one of this country's first great artists, Charles Willson Peale. Peale was interested in his sitter's longevity—Mamout claimed to be 133 years old at the time. But the artist's diary, one of only two available recognizable descriptions of Mamout, shows that Peale became quite interested in the man for other reasons as well. He had him sit two days, longer than he had planned, was pleased with their conversation, and talked to the white family that knew Mamout's history. The husband of Mrs. Bell freed him in April 1807. She said Mamout was about fourteen when purchased, not thirty five as he claimed. She admitted, however, that she could have been mistaken.

mistaken. Mamout was always a good worker, she said, and after he made the bricks for the Bells' large house in Georgetown, Maryland, he was set free. Ever enterprising, he twice survived losses of his earnings to whites but eventually bought a house and lot and was a kind of character around town. He enjoyed a "good temper" even when local boys teased him and was known for his "sobriety and a cheerful conduct," his Muslim prayers in the streets, and his jocular way with local businessmen. After about a century in America, he still adhered to the religion of his youth and to its dietary restrictions, saying, "It is no good to eat hog—& drink whiskey is very bad." The religion had preserved the man, apparently. He seems to have been illiterate; no writings have been passed on. There are also no indications that he chose to have a family in America.

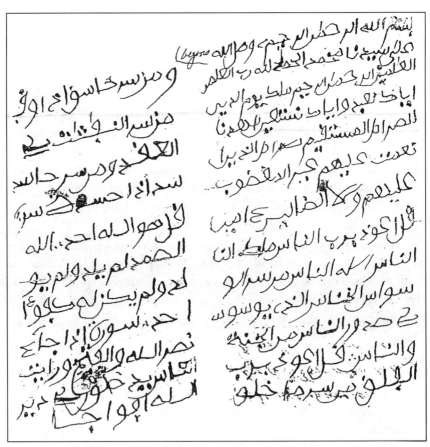

Fig. 7.   Fatiha, Surahs 114—the Last, 113, 112, 110 by "a Negro Slave of Capt. **David** Anderson," South Carolina, 1768. Savannah Historical Society.

quotations Peale provides suggest that Mamout did not strive to learn the language of the unbelievers around him. Perhaps he was not as happy as he appeared to be.

Most of those Africans who were brought to New Orleans in the eighteenth century—the period studied by Gwendolyn Midlo Hall in her book *Africans in Colonial Louisiana*—recognized that they were brought from ports in Senegal and the Gambia. These people would all later be called, lazily, Mandingoes by such writers on that city as George Washington Cable. Hall lists in Appendix D twenty-eight names that appear to be Muslim. It is possible that a few of these people were not Muslims; it is also undoubtedly true that many slaves listed by non-Muslim names given to them by their masters had had Muslim names given to them by their parents. Hall wrote that the French paid attention to the populations they brought to America. They were after people familiar with rice and indigo raising, and, apparently, they wanted people with Muslim training as they presumed their belief in one god, in prayer, in the powers of those who could read, and in the dignity conveyed with their covering their bodies made them superior to non-Muslims as managers. When Americans began to carry slaves themselves at the end of the century, they continued to prefer Senegambians to all others for Louisiana and other colonies—undoubtedly for similar reasons. More recognition of African Muslims will come from present and future studies of peculiarly American postindependence slave-carrying and -importing practices from the 1780s to the 1860s.

In 1768, a "negro slave of Capt. David Anderson" (hereafter Anderson's Negro), somewhere in South Carolina, otherwise unidentified, wrote selections from the Quran. His two-page manuscript in Arabic includes, in the following order, Surahs (chapters) 1, 114 (the last), 113, 112—the most important, worth a third of the Quran, as translator William Brown Hodgson said in 1838—and 110 (the first half; another page or more has been lost). Essentially, these pages reassert the faith of the writer.

Jupiter Dowda, a Hausa, probably from present-day Nigeria, worked on the Mississippi River for a slave trader but died a freeman in Philadelphia, where his owners wrote in 1800 that in twenty years of working for them, "he never did a base thing, told a falsehood, got intoxicated or swore an oath." He took a wife in America, but there is no mention of her religion or of children.

Big Jack, called a Mandingo, was used as an overseer by a slave trader from Natchez, Mississippi at about the same time.

Abd ar-Rahman came across a handful of Muslims near Natchez; he also met one in Hartford, Connecticut.

Sambo, probably originally Samba—a second son—who wrote "the Arabic language," absconded with three other "new Negroes" in 1805. Obviously a Muslim, he may have been trying to run back to Africa. Historian Michael A. Gomez has found a dozen Muslim names from around the last turn of the century in fugitive slave advertisements. Two fled from the plantation of Bilali's master, Thomas Spalding of Sapelo Island, Georgia. Gomez has also found as many Muslim names in slave lists in an ongoing investigation.

In December 1807, the last month Americans were able to legally import Africans, a massive man was allowed to come out of the filthy hold of a slave ship in Charleston, South Carolina, but hog-tied and under heavy guard. S'Quash, as he was called, was, according to descendants of his purchasers, a superior type; an excellent horseman; a slave trader; literate in Arabic; an eventual plantation manager; and, though "extremely dark," "obviously not a Negro." White reporters, faced with intelligent, self-respecting blacks, often found it necessary to deny the latters' Africanness, as is illustrated often in this book, especially in the cases of Abd ar-Rahman, Umar ibn Said, and other people met by Joel Chandler Harris. Adhering to such myths, whites asserted that S'Quash held himself aloof from "Negroes" and did not marry until a Dinka (Sudanese—very unlikely) woman was found whom he thought fitting despite her brown color—again according to descendants of his masters. The more likely reason is that he wanted a Muslim wife. Their children, as wonderful as their parents, were the property of Joseph Graham. After Graham's death, S'Quash helped other Grahams to settle slaves in distant Mississippi. A portrait was made of this pleasing slave, but its present whereabouts are unknown.

The quote in Chapter 1 of a slave declaring that the first whites the speaker ever saw were ugly—showing a healthy ethnocentrism—issued from a "man who prayed five times a day," though he was in South Carolina. This man was the only one of the narrators to provide details on the horrors of his Atlantic crossing. He was also the only one to have an African American interviewer. Surely there is a connection. European American interviewers usually chose not to ask about this experience or to skip rapidly over it with sentimental remarks. This man's nineteen-page story comes from the slave narrative of Charles Ball, who appears to be the only American slave autobiographer who came across a Muslim and recognized him. In fact, Ball was so impressed with this man's heartfelt praying that he was moved to contrast it to what he called the superstitions, including Christian ones, that his fellow slaves were victims of in South Carolina, where masters had "a strong repugnance against their slaves becoming members of any religious society." They feared that slaves might learn something about "equality and liberty."

This man (hereafter Ball's Muslim), a Tuareg, perhaps, and a Muslim, told of desert wandering and warfare in what is probably now Mali, "a country, which had no trees, nor grass upon it," and of being enslaved by enemy Muslims who made him take care of camels and goats. He then told of a long adventure with two lions, occurring not long before his capture by non-Muslims, probably Bambaras. He was marched to the Gambia River, where he witnessed the casting overboard of three babies whose mothers leaped after them, and told of many suffering and many dying from the heat in the ship on the river and of its tight-packed load. Food was carelessly distributed, and one-third of those aboard died before their arrival in Charleston, South Carolina, probably in 1807. He was not able to stand or straighten his limbs for a week after this terrible voyage. Ball's Muslim could tell a story, and it is unfortunate that nothing more has been discovered about him.

Another proud, self-respecting Muslim quoted in Chapter 1 was the unnamed, outspoken "Moorish slave" (hereafter the "Moor"), who was interviewed in 1822, ten years after being brought illegally to work on the Mississippi River. He declared that his homeland was more comfortable and his people more learned than what he had seen in America. He wrote the Fatiha (opening chapter of the Quran) in Arabic for his white interviewer—and who knows what else he might have written had he been urged and had he seen any benefit in doing so?—and told some of his history. Before being taken away, he had been the son of a Muslim prince on the Niger River. With a "small body of men," he had made an incursion into enemy territory and was captured, taken to the coast, and put on a Spanish ship that took him to New Orleans. "He has one wife"—presumably in America. His sympathetic interviewer—a trader in pork, by the way—said the man "lamented in terms of bitter regret, that his situation as a slave in America, prevents him from obeying the dictates of his religion. He is under the necessity of eating pork, but denies ever tasting any kind of spirits." Clearly the "Moor" strove to adhere to his religion, and ten years of American slavery had not made him think worse of Africa and Islam.

Charno and Tombo are African Muslim slaves in a semiautobiographical novel *The Kentuckian in New York* (1834), and Sylvia, a female Muslim, appears in the same author's *Knights of the Golden Horseshoe,* by William A. Caruthers. They appear to be based on real people. "Charno" sounds very much like *chierno* or *thierno*, pronunciations of a title designating a literate Fula. Charno wrote the Fatiha, or opening chapter of the Quran (see this book's frontispiece), for the narrator, who had it properly translated. Caruthers told a little of the writer's history.

The document was gained in the following way:

> "I asked if any of those present could write; they replied that there was one man in the quarter who could write in his own language, and several of them went out and brought in a tall, bald-headed old fellow, who seemed to come with great reluctance. After being told what was desired, he acknowledged to me that he could write when he last tried, which was many years previous. I took out my pocket-book, tore out a blank leaf, and handing him a pen from my pocket inkstand, requested him to give me a specimen. He took the head of the barrel on his lap, and began, if I recollect right, on the right side of the page."

Caruthers provided "a facsimile of his performance" and "a liberal translation into English"—it is a decent one:

> "In the name of God the merciful! the compassionate! God bless our Lord Mohammed his prophet, and his descendants, and his followers, and prosper them exceedingly. Praise be to God the Lord of all creatures! the merciful, the compassionate king of the day of judgment! Thee we adore, and of thee we implore assistance! Guide us in the right way, the way of those with whom thou art well pleased, and not of those with whom thou art angry, nor of those who are in error. Amen!" The original is written in Arabic. The old fellow's name is Charno, which it seems he has retained, after being enslaved, contrary to their general custom in that respect. I became quite affected and melancholy in talking to this venerable old man, and you may judge from that rare circumstance that he is no common character.

But Caruthers did not take this too seriously: "I now fixed my saddle under my head in a cotton shed to rest for the night; but, weary as I was, I could not directly get to sleep for thinking of sandy deserts, old Charno, chicken suppers, negro quarters, and Virginia Bell! You see she is still the heroine, let my wanderings lay the scenes where they will."

The author's wife had a Muslim slave called Bullutah (Bilali?).

In 1825 the secretary of the American Colonization Society (ACS), R. R. Gurley writing in its journal, *The African Repository*, recalled having heard of a number of Muslims in American slavery.

Very little has been found on other Muslim slaves. Southerner Joseph LeConte remembered

an old African, named Philip, who was a very intelligent man. He used to tell us about the customs and religion of the country from which he came. He was not a pagan, but a Mohammedan [Muslim]. He greatly interested us by going through all the prayers and prostrations of his native country. He also gave us the numerals up to twenty: These were, of course, native African, not Arabic. They were "go, dede, tata, nigh, ja, jago, jadal, jatata, ja nigh, suppe, suppe ja, suppa jago, suppa ja dede, suppa ja tata, suppa ja nigh." It is seen that they count by fives and not by tens as we do.

It would be interesting to know how LeConte knew as much as he thought he did, and why he did not learn more from Philip. The numerals identify Philip as another Fula.

After years of slavery in Tennessee, Hamet Abdul—obviously a man who had insisted on his Muslim name—sought money to return to Africa. He was noticed in 1834.

A character named King, who seems to be based upon a real person, appears in another semiautobiographical novel, *The Planter, or Thirteen Years in the South* by one David Brown (1853). King is described as having the "dignity of a retired field marshall and the authority of a patriarch," and locals liked to say that he had converted from Islam to Christianity. But there is some question in the mind of the narrator about this conversion. There is none, however, about using King's virtues to disparage by comparison the "uncivilizable purely negro race" of other slaves on the plantation. African Muslims, to the narrator, were mingled breeds, only a little further advanced than the "purely negro" slaves. He was echoing, of course, the philosophic-scientific thinkers of his day—a day whose sun has not completely set even in 1996.

I am assuming an Islamic identity for the runaway Osman (probably Usuman) whose dramatic portrait follows. Encountered in the 1850s, he quickly slid back into his Virginia swamp after being visible only for a moment. But the artist, David H. Strother, had clearly been moved:

About thirty paces from me I saw a gigantic negro, with a tattered blanket wrapped about his shoulders, and a gun in his hand. His head was bare, and he had little other clothing than a pair of ragged breeches and boots. His hair and beard were tipped with gray, and his purely African features were cast

Fig. 8. Osman [Usuman?], Runaway in Great Dismal Swamp, North Carolina, 1852, Porte Crayon (pseud. David H. Strother), *The Old South Illustrated*, 1856, p. 148.

in a mould betokening, in the highest degree, strength and energy. The expression of the face was of mingled fear and ferocity, and every movement betrayed a life of habitual caution and watchfulness. He reached forward his iron hand to clear away the brier screen that half concealed him while it interrupted his scrutinizing glance, fortunately, he did not discover me, but presently turned and disappeared.

A later article in the *Raleigh News and Observer* (August 3, 1913) attempted to tell more. Written from Edenton, it said Osman was "a famous African chief, who was sold into slavery but escaped" into the Great Dismal Swamp. He there "led a reign of terror during the early fifties. He obtained firearms," became "half wild, and was credited with the power of speech with snakes and animals of the forest and cypress swamps." Posses were sent to find him but failed. Tradition "is fast fixed in the minds of the negroes and swamp settlers that Osman accidentally stepped upon a coiled body of a cottonmouth moccasin and died a few minutes later in dreadful agony." Negroes claim still to hear "the scream of Osman's ghost re-enacting the death struggle."

This tale's hero seems to share the animal-speaking talent of Joel Chandler Harris's Aaron. But Osman, unlike Aaron, is hostile to whites and slavery.

A Georgia slave, London, removed to Florida in the 1850s shortly before he died, deserves recognition for his truly extraordinary efforts in Arabic. His manuscripts provided problems to the translator, William Brown Hodgson, until he discovered that London had done what thousands of West Africans had done before him: written the local language with Arabic characters. Once he gave up looking for Arabic vocabulary and transliterated London's letters into sounds, he came up with the following:

> Fas chapta ob jon.
> Inde be ginnen wasde wad;
> ande Wad waswid Gad,
> ande wad was Gad.

This slave was putting the Gospel into his American language. He had also done the same for some hymns, according to Hodgson. Thus far, unhappily, the originals of these potential linguistic treasures have not been found. It is also impossible to know whether London was doing this writing out of a broad spiritual interest or because he had converted to Christianity. Hodgson owned a Muslim slave, but that man could not write Arabic.

One might wonder whether London was trying to meld the two religions. According to the Georgia preacher-historian Charles Colcock Jones, who offered no numbers, some slaves were "known to accommodate Christianity to Mohammedanism." "'God,' say they, 'is Allah, and Jesus Christ is Mohammed—the religion is the same, but different countries have different names.'" Perhaps this merging occurred, but as we shall see, few Muslims appear to have done it. There is, however, a pronouncement by the lone Muslim woman to be quoted in that period that supports Jones's conclusion. "Old Lizzy Gray," recently dead in South Carolina according to a report in 1860, had been educated in "Mahomedan tenets," and though she had latterly been considered a Methodist, "she ever said that Christ built the first church in Mecca and he grave was da." She had done some wild combining. Muhammad made Mecca the chief city in Islam, and his tomb is in Jerusalem.

This is not the only such combination, however; a similar accommodation emerged in 1913 when a black North Carolinian named Timothy Drew—whose origins are obscure—founded the Moorish Science Temple, in which Allah was God, Jesus his prophet.

It is also true, of course, that some Africans were Muslimized to varying degrees. To say, "There is no God but Allah, and Muhammad is his prophet," was enough to save one from slavery in some Old World times and places.

A post–Civil War incident of an African Muslim in antebellum America was recalled in the 1890s. A Miss Leach wrote to Joel Chandler Harris (who once wrote that "Arabic-Africans" along the coast of Georgia were "not the most numerous, but the most noticeable" type) to tell him about her great-grandfather's one-time slave Aaron. He was an Arab (she said) with a personality that cowed black and white alike. At some point, Aaron had boldly declared that he wanted no more of slavery and was allowed, even helped with his master's money, to walk away from it to Canada. From there, from time to time, he wrote properly respectful yet independent letters to his former owner. Nothing more has been discovered about this man.

Let me widen the picture at this point. Since "American" may be understood as naming all the nations in the New World, available glimpses of African Muslims on nearby shores are also informative. An unnamed Mandingo servant who could write the Arabic language "with great beauty and exactness" was owned by a historian of the West Indies, Bryan Edwards, who knew of at least one other such servant nearby in Jamaica near the turn of the eighteenth century. A fortunate Mohammed, enslaved in 1798, was freed in 1811 and returned to Africa by his master in Antigua precisely because of his attachment to Islam.

Mohammed Kaba, once a merchant in Africa; William Rainsford, a forceful preacher from Kankan (present-day Guinea); Charles Larten, a Quranic expert; Anna Mousa, or Benjamin Cochrane, a medical doctor from Mali; and the geographically knowledgeable Abu Bakr as-Siddiq, all literate, all forced into unwanted baptisms in Jamaica (where half the imports may have been from the Senegambia to the Gold Coast and hinterlands from which Muslims would have been drawn), told significant and touching stories about their lives and their shared religion. Unfortunately, only Richard Robert Madden, an Irish abolitionist who in 1833 was one of six special magistrates mandated to oversee the ultimate liberation of the newly freed slaves in Jamaica, seems to have paid attention to these Muslims. Having had some experience with the Arabic language in Arabia, he became interested in the authors of Arabic writings on the island.

Once he gained their trust, they told about a turn-of-the-century circulating letter in Arabic that was an exhortation to remain pure and faithful. Rainsford wrote a sermon, concluding with a declaration that the rich had a duty to not oppress the poor; Larten wrote out the Quran from memory; Mousa wrote one or two short autobiographies; and Abu Bakr composed a wonderful autobiography and list of trade routes in West Africa—all in Arabic. Madden did his best to translate them.

Abu Bakr was from a sophisticated, wealthy, and extensive Mandingo trading family. Born in Timbuktu around 1794, he was a student—and apparently a good one—until sometime in 1807, when he was captured because he was on the losing side in a war. The autobiography is very informative about his family, their trading ventures, and the conflict that led to his enslavement in what is now Ghana. A second translator of his autobiography, George C. Renouard, who spent time with Abu Bakr in London in 1835, was very impressed by the man's intelligence and geographical knowledge. Abu Bakr reported that he had visited or heard about towns from Sin near the mouth of the Gambia to Katsina in Nigeria, more than 1,600 miles to the east, and from Timbuktu to the Guinea coast, about 900 miles to the south. He went further and told Renouard of their geographical relationships to one another. He was laying out an area comparable in size to the United States east of the Mississippi. Not many Americans would have been able to lay out similar lists. Abu Bakr also described a vast and apparently active network of communities reaching through and beyond many different peoples. There were undoubtedly Muslims in each community.

Renouard was also impressed with Abu Bakr's faith, which is concisely and touchingly expressed in the conclusion to his autobiography:

The faith of our families is the faith of Islám. They circumcise the foreskin; say the five prayers; fast every year in the month of Ramadán; give alms as ordained in the law; marry (only) four free women—[others are] forbidden to them except she be their slave; they fight for the faith of God; perform the pilgrimage (to Mecca)—*i.e.* such as are able to do so; eat the flesh of no beast but what they have slain for themselves; drink no wine—or whatever intoxicates is forbidden unto them; they do not keep company with those whose faith is contrary to theirs,—such as worshippers of idols, men who swear falsely by the name of the Lord, who dishonour their parents, commit murder or robbery, bear false witness, are covetous, proud, insolent hypocrites, unclean in their discourse, or do any other thing that is forbidden; they teach their children to read, and (instruct them in) the different parts of knowledge; their minds are perfect and blameless according to the measure of their faith.

Abu Bakr added the poignant note: "Verily, I have erred and done wickedly, but I entreat God to guide my heart in the right path, for He knoweth what is in my heart, and whatever (can be pleaded) in my behalf."

A few months later, Abu Bakr was chosen by a self-proclaimed explorer, John Davidson, to guide a private expedition from Morocco's Atlantic port of Wadi Nun to Timbuktu. Davidson and his men were killed before they got far, but two years later a report said that Abu Bakr had returned to the famous city of Jenne and to some part of his family.

(Hereafter these Jamaican Africans will be referred to as Kaba, Rainsford, Cochrane, and Abu Bakr.)

Renouard, Abu Bakr's British translator, was also to find that the famous Amistad slave ship rebels led by Cinque in 1839 were familiar with Muslim salutations, and one claimed to be the son of a *marabout,* or Muslim "priest."

Recent studies by João José Reis of the major slave revolt in Bahia, Brazil (1835), put Muslims back in the forefront. Paul E. Lovejoy found rebels who were active both in their Nigerian homelands and in Brazil, providing more specifics about the presence and prestige of Muslims that appear to support the controversial arguments of Gilberto Freyre that Muslims were politically and culturally influential in Brazil. Lovejoy is also studying the nineteenth-century trade of Muslims between Brazil and Africa.

Though his work has a less broad scale than Freyre's, Carlton R. Ottley dedicated his history *Slavery Days in Trinidad* to "Mandingo Africans" who banded together in a Free Mandingo Society to ransom fellow Muslims from slavery in his island country. Ottley reported that in a petition to King William some of the members stated their unhappiness over the way their own non-

Muslim slaves were acting, but they also told of keeping up their African custom of treating their slaves as working wards: They ate at the same tables and slept in the same houses. Here is a picture not of American but of African slavery. Further, Ottley mentioned that in 1816 about one thousand West Indian regimentals who had been "recruited" in the American South during the War of 1812 went to the West Indies and that about 240 were converted to Islam by members of the society; some of these may have come from Salih Bilali's St. Simon's Island—see Chapter 5.

One of the members of this society was the subject of a biography. Mohamedu Sisei was kidnapped from the banks of the Gambia, but his ship was caught by a craft from a British anti-slavery squadron. Along with other able-bodied Africans, he was "released" and signed up by the British for seven, then fourteen, years of service in H.M. West Indian Regiments. There he naturally met Africans from many nations who were converting to Islam in the early nineteenth century. He mentions a regiment's conversion and a successful petition requesting a return to Africa. I have not been able to corroborate this story yet.

Finally, on Cuba, the Swedish novelist and traveler Fredrika Bremer decided that Mandingoes were the "preachers and fortune tellers" of the blacks.

The roll call of known African Muslims goes this far to date. I am confident other names and stories will reappear to further fill out the picture.

We may begin here to sketch a composite.

Except for Baquaqua and Ball's Muslim, who were servants of non-Muslim and of Muslim chiefs, respectively, each of the narrators had been in Africa a professional or learned man or student. One may have been an heir to a "kingdom" (ar-Rahman); he and at least one other (Cochrane) were also soldiers with extensive campaigning experience. A possible future *imam* or religious-political leader was also a trader (Job), as were two others who were also teachers (Kebe and Umar—and possibly the Moor from the Mississippi River); often the three professions went together. (For a modern description of a Muslim teacher, see Cheikh Hamidou Kane, *Ambiguous Adventure*, 1963.) Also represented here are a "linguister," or translator (Jay), a medical doctor (Cochrane), a student of law (Bilali), and at least four other students who had been moving up to advanced studies (Abu Bakr, Rainsford, Benjamin Larten, Said, and probably the Moor on the Mississippi). The professions of the others are not known, but each apparently received some special training. Only one admitted to not being interested in studying or in blacksmithing—Baquaqua again. All appear to have come from prominent families, and all seem to have been preparing to lead lives in which their communities might take pride.

These men were all Africans. Represented here are five who identified themselves as Fulbe because they had Fulbe fathers: Job, ar-Rahman, Bilali, Salih Bilali (whose master's description fits the classic Mandingo), and Umar (a Tukolor—as is novelist Kane). Philip's numbers and Charno's name suggest they were Fulbe. They came from the darker side of this ethnically interesting people—and, contrary to white ethnologists' common assumptions, usually the more scholarly and urban, "civilized" side. Five of the men were identified as being "Mandingoes": Mohammed Kaba; Rainsford; Abu Bakr (whose mother was a Hausa); and, according to their master's guesses, Anderson's Negro, King, and London. Baquaqua had a Songhai father and a Hausa mother; Cochrane was a Kassonke; Kebe was a Soninke or Serahule who had a "Manenca" (Mandingo) mother; and Said had a Kanuri father and a Mandara mother. Portraits exist of Job, Yarrow Mamout, ar-Rahman, Umar, Baquaqua, Said, and Osman. Images of Mamout and Osman are reproduced in this chapter; others are included in relevant chapters. Photographs of some of the grand-children of Bilali and Salih Bilali also exist, and two are reproduced below.

The experiences of these people offer glimpses of ten African homelands, their commerce, and the influence and depth of West African Islam during more than a century of the trade in African lives. But with their captures, their power, family connections, and hopes were cut forever—with the exception of Job and Jay, perhaps, who returned to Africa within a decade of being taken away. However, these people's intellectual, spiritual, and psychological acquirements were not cut off, as we have seen.

The travels of these men as captives from two hundred to one thousand miles inland to the shores of Africa varied, of course. Job, Jay, ar-Rahman, and Ball's Muslim were shipped from the Gambia River. Umar and probably Yarrow, King, and Cochrane were sent down the Senegal River. Bilali, Kebe, and Rainsford were probably shipped out of the Kaba River of Guinea. Salih Bilali passed through Mali and the Ivory Coast via powerful empire-building Bambarans and Ashanti; Baquaqua was passed on by slave-hustling Dahomeans of Benin. Abu Bakr was taken from the land of the independent Mossi of Burkina Faso, south through Ghana. Said was taken in the other direction, across the Sahara, through the Tuareg-Arabic lands of Niger and Libya.

Apparently only Baquaqua and Ball's Muslim were asked about, or cared to tell of, their Middle Passage experiences. This is a disappointing omission, of course. However, ar-Rahman's modern biographer, Terry Alford, was able to find out a great deal about the very ships in which his subject was transported across the Atlantic to Dominica and thence to New Orleans.

The qualities these men brought with them presented problems to buyers:

People from educated, professional, and once free classes had to be handled with care. They had special antipathies toward physical labor and, naturally, toward their enslavement, as is clear from the narratives of Abu Bakr, Job Ben Solomon, ar-Rahman, Umar ibn Said, and Mohammed Ali ben Said, or Nicholas Said. Across America they posed distinct problems and dangers. In the folklore of Mexico, Uruguay, Venezuela, and Argentina, "mandinga" meant "sorcerer."

In these narratives and notes there are barely tapped sources for modern historians interested in African adjustments to the New World's callous demands. They do not need to wonder about the first responses and experiences of several of these narrators in America. We know that eleven were sent out to work in the fields, as one might expect: Job, Jay, and Yarrow Mamout in Maryland; Bilali and Salih Bilali in the Bahamas and then to Georgia; ar-Rahman in Spanish Mississippi; Umar for a short time in South Carolina before he was purchased by a man who saved him from manual labor in North Carolina; Kebe in three states in the South; Kaba and Abu Bakr in Jamaica; and Baquaqua in Brazil. Cochrane fought for British West India regiments and on British battleships, and Baquaqua was put to work on a ship to New York.

At least three were wholly or partly successful runaways. Job and Umar were caught and imprisoned; Job was returned to a chastened master after being promised lighter labor because he had proved to be literate. Umar persuaded someone other than his distant, mean second purchaser to ransom him and to treat him gently for the rest of his long life. Ar-Rahman stayed away for a while but eventually turned himself in for reasons he seems to have kept to himself. Others, including Osman and people referred to in fugitive slave ads ran away often. Each seems to have been treated somewhat better after having run, if he had to return.

Six became longtime plantation managers: ar-Rahman was a power from around 1800 to 1818 near Natchez. Bilali was often the sole manager for his master, who ultimately owned Sapelo Island; his friend, Salih Bilali, held a similar position on St. Simon's Island, Georgia, after 1816. Some time later, King managed a plantation in Georgia, S'Quash one in South Carolina. Abu Bakr was manager of a Jamaican plantation. Perhaps the prestige they enjoyed, or the fear they inspired—stories abound of both—or their authoritative ways as former members of elites helped them gain such positions. Ar-Rahman had been a leader of men on the battlefield. Kebe, Umar, and perhaps Bilali were used to ordering students around, and a few of these men may have been overseers of agricultural slave gangs at home. They had to assert themselves in certain ways to get these positions, of course, and some of the accommodations made by their American masters are discussed later. Bilali and Salih Bilali became at least locally famous for their efforts at keeping their slaves from running to the British during the War of 1812 and for saving them in the notorious hurricane of 1824.

Surely the literacy of many, outlined on pages 23 and 24 above, helped them keep the faith. Their writings were listed at the end of Chapter 1.

Apparently only Nicholas Said ever learned to write English well. Seven letters in English in Baquaqua's hand show that he was trying—and that he was beginning late. Several narrators told about another kind of writing, about Africans using Arabic script for local-language documents, like London and Abu Bakr.

The records show that four of the narrators—Job, Mamout, Bilali, and Salih Bilali—practiced their public praying according to Quranic obligations despite ridicule and other pressures. The Moor on the Mississippi regretted that he was forced to eat pork, but he said he kept up with other Muslim rules. Ar-Rahman, Kebe, and Baquaqua promised to preach Christianity if they could return to Africa, but in each case it is clear that their serious goals were only to return. Ar-Rahman reverted to Islam as soon as he saw the coast of Africa again; the same may be assumed about Kebe, as his statements herein suggest; Baquaqua's reputed conversion is barely mentioned in his biography-autobiography. Five Muslims were obliged to undergo baptism in Jamaica, but each declared that the act had been involuntary. Their true faiths were discovered easily by their common amanuensis. Indeed, Abu Bakr's autobiography declares his chagrin at not being a perfect Muslim. Nicholas Said had not understood the meaning of his baptism in Russia. Only London, in his writing of the Gospel of John, and King, Umar, Baquaqua, and Said, in statements that Christians took to be conclusive and any Muslim would take to be political—or wise, as some Christian prayers such as the Lord's Prayer or the Twenty-third Psalm are no more Christian than Muslim—seem to have seriously suggested conversion.

There were other ways to accommodate themselves. Mamout worked out his freedom and became a small landowner and local character in Georgetown, D.C. Umar became a pampered slave by convincing his new master that he was unhealthy. The poor fellow then managed to survive for more than half a century as a storyteller and apparent Oriental saint to neighbors and visitors from near and far. Cochrane became a respected doctor in Jamaica. Baquaqua studied to become a missionary. Seven at least, including two of the runaways (Job and ar-Rahman), gained passage to Africa.

Where anything is known about the immediate families of these men, we know that Job and Jay's persistence paid off: They went home to their African families—although one of Job's wives had remarried. As far as American families are concerned, Rahman probably had some struggles with his Baptist wife over the religious upbringing of their children, but she and five children did go to Africa. Bilali and Salih Bilali—who had several wives—bequeathed Muslim names and traditions to their American offspring that their descendants recalled late in the 1930s. It appears that Mamout, Kebe, and Umar decided against bringing children into the world as they found it; there is no record that they had American children.

Like other Africans in the New World, African American Muslim children probably had to adapt to their new religious and sociopolitical environments, as have other hyphenated Americans. Little is known about the children of these Muslims. But there are two known examples, and both are impressive, of second-generation Muslim families. Both are in Georgia's Sea Islands and related to Bilali and Salih Bilali. It is possible there were more.

Too few were noticed by too many. Information about Captain Anderson's literate servant and London was found only in the papers of the slaveholder-scholar William Brown Hodgson, to whom the biography of Salih Bilali was sent. The self-sustaining Yarrow Mamout, the outspoken Moor on the Mississippi, the stern King, the quiet Charno, Kebe, Ball's Muslim who persistently prayed five times a day, and others each had only one or two whites who thought them worthy of written attention, and usually not in widely disseminated papers. Accordingly, no one advertised the considerable managerial capabilities or the heroic activities in the War of 1812 of Bilali and Salih Bilali, and no one elaborated on the Muslim communities these two created in Georgia's Sea Islands. There was no virtue in going far afield, of course, to recognize the impressively literate and informed Jamaican or Trinidadian Muslim communities.

It is difficult to tell what the relations of these people were to non-Muslims because most of the commentators were white. Nearly all of these whites liked to think that they despised so-called animists and nappy-haired, presumably blacker Africans. Such writers tried hard to depict Job, ar-Rahman, S'Quash, Umar, King, and others as antiblack. These Muslims undoubtedly did feel superior to non-Muslims, but this attitude included whites too. Ibrahim Abd ar-Rahman married a black woman, as did S'Quash. Black Charles Ball did not tell that his Muslim acquaintance stayed aloof from blacks. Quite daringly, ar-Rahman, dependent on the kindness of white strangers from whom he was seeking money from Washington, D.C., to Boston, Massachusetts, met with African Americans in Boston, New York, and Philadelphia. Those blacks who spoke of him did not find him someone who despised them. In North Carolina there were blacks who may have understood Umar better than white Christians. They knew him as a religious man and as a "pray-god to the king"—a Muslim religious adviser to a non-Muslim. Umar may have played a comparable role with his American neighbors.

As noted above, several of these narrators felt free to offer opinions on America and Christianity. Undoubtedly, few available reports say exactly what the narrator would have said had he composed his story on his own or with a wholly trusted editor—therefore, these reports are not to be considered complete or final. Many contemporary sources of information on these people come from reports of meetings of and writings by American Colonization Society members and sympathizers—many of whom were primitive ethnologists and one a gifted linguist—in various issues of colonization newspapers, pamphlets, letters, and an occasional book. Other sources are important city, state, and federal officials: two mayors, a congressman, a secretary of state, and President John Quincy Adams; ministers hoping to convert Muslims into Christians; two travelers' accounts; three novelists' pages; a magazine editor; several newspaper editors—including one African American; Thomas Gallaudet, the founder of the first school for the hearing impaired; the writings of only one active abolitionist—an Irishman in Jamaica; an autobiography by an eventual Civil War soldier published in the prestigious *Atlantic Monthly* in 1867; the diary of a great American painter, Charles Willson Peale; and one excerpt from a slave narrative. Nor are all the documents available. Further documents remain to be found, and more information remains to be discovered about these figures as individuals, as representatives of their African and Afro-American peers, as informants on their times and places and conditions, and as storytellers speaking for otherwise unrecorded millions.

SELECTED READINGS

For the "man who prayed five times a day," see *Slavery in the United States: A Narrative of the Life and Adventures of Charles Ball, a Black Man*, 3rd ed. (1st ed. 1836; Pittsburgh: Shyrock, 1854), 142–161.

For S'Quash, see *The Natural Bent: The Memoirs of Dr. Paul B. Barringer.* (Chapel Hill: University of North Carolina Press, 1949). Brought to my attention by Thomas Parramore.

For King, see [David Brown], *The Planter, or Thirteen Years in the South— by a Northern Man* (Philadelphia: Hooker, 1853), 100–128, 141.

For Osman, see Porte Crayon (pseudonym for David H. Strother), *The Old South Illustrated* (1856) (reprinted Chapel Hill: University of North Carolina Press, 1959), 146–148.

For Charno and other Muslim characters in Caruthers, see Curtis Carroll Davis, *Chronicler of the Cavaliers: A Life of the Virginia Novelist, Dr. William A. Caruthers* (Richmond, Va.: Dietz, 1953), 50, 344–347, 504–505, 92–104.

Gwendolyn Midlo Hall, *Africans in Colonial Louisiana: The Development of Afro-Creole Culture in the 18th Century.* Baton Rouge: Louisiana State University Press, 1992.

For London, see William Brown Hodgson (1801–1879), "The Gospels, Written in the Negro Patois of English, with Arabic Characters, by a Mandingo Slave in Georgia" (New York: [American Ethnological Society?], 1857), 5, 10. Hodgson also referred to Muslims writing Spanish with Arabic characters, p. 4.

For David Anderson's literate "Negro," see William Brown Hodgson, "Letter to John Vaughan," Philadelphia, November 3, 1838, W. B. Hodgson Papers, Savannah Historical Society, Misc. Oriental Mss. Brought to my attention by Muhammad al-Ahari.

For Yarrow Mamout, see Sidney and Emma N. Kaplan, *The Black Presence in the Era of the American Revolution, 1770–1800* (Amherst: University of Massachusetts Press, 1993). A second portrait exists, by James Alexander Simpson, Georgetown Branch, D.C. Public Library.

For Abu Bakr as-Siddiq, Mohammed Kaba, William Rainsford, Benjamin Larten, and Anna Mousa, see Richard Robert Madden, *A Twelve Month's Residence in the West Indies During the Transition from Slavery to Apprenticeship, with Incidental Notices of the State of Society, Prospects, and Natural Resources of Jamaica and Other Islands* (Philadelphia: Carey, Lea, and Blanchard, 1835). T[homas] Davidson, ed. *Notes Taken During Travels in Africa* (London: privately printed, 1839). "Routes in North Africa by Abu Baker es Siddik," trans. G[eorge] C. Renouard, *Journal of the Royal Geographical Society* VI (1836), 99–113.

Carlton Ottley, *Slavery Days in Trinidad: A Social History of the Island from 1797–1838* (Trinidad: the author, 1974).

For the "Moor on the Mississippi," see Thomas A. Teas, "A Trading Trip to Natchez and New Orleans, 1822 (Diary)," *Journal of Southern History* 7 (1941), 378–399. Brought to my attention by Sidney Kaplan.

Fig. 9. Job Ben Solomon, Oil Painting by William Hoare, England, 1733, photo courtesy of Sidney Kaplan.

3

Job Ben Solomon:
African Nobleman and a Father
of African American Literature

Job Ben Solomon Jallo (the most common version of his name in English and American publications) was no more deserving or extraordinary than many other Africans enslaved in the New World—including other Fulbes such as Yarrow (Jallo?) Mamout (Mohammed) and Charno (Chierno) from Chapter 2, Ibrahim Abd ar-Rahman Jallo from Chapter 4, Bilali Muhammad and Salih Bilali from Chapter 5, and Umar ibn Said of Chapter 7. But he was more fortunate because he was freed after less than three years of slavery in America.

When Job appeared before surprised and sympathetic Europeans, prior to the rise of both antislavery and antiblack theories, his impressive manner and mind and his strong African and Muslim identity attracted the serious attention of a number of colonial Marylanders and old-country Englishmen. One of the latter was his future friend and biographer Thomas Bluett, whom he met in 1732, the year George Washington was born. By 1734, about the same time the English were becoming the leading carriers of Africans into New World slavery, Job gained the enthusiastic assistance of several of England's wealthiest, most sophisticated, and most influential leaders, who arranged and eased with gifts and money his unusual return to Africa as a free man. Further, he became an important commercial agent as a Royal African Company (RAC) trader and a protector of his own people because he was given the right to ransom fellow Muslims brought to the Company for sale.

Though telling his story was no longer crucial to his own well-being, but potentially valuable to others like him and to those "ignorant of Africa" then and now, Job authorized a memoir by his English friend Thomas Bluett that was published the year he returned to Africa. This work was the first "life and thoughts" of a sub-Saharan African in a European language. Retellings of Job's story from that time to ours, in fact, have helped keep Job relatively famous internationally. Few books on Africa in the slave trade era fail to mention this reportedly well-mannered, even courtly, monotheistic, and literate human being. But few have explored his significance and many have transformed him, because of his literacy in Arabic and their author's antiblack prejudices, into a Moor or Arab. Neither his amazing history nor his book, despite the primacy of the latter, had the healthy effect they might have had on images of Africans.

Instead of reading his life and his memoir as the history of a representative, intelligent, clearly civilized man trained in Africa, many writers have retold his adventures as the history of an unusual, not quite African individual saved by English generosity. Instead of one of Africa's noblemen, Job was transformed into one of Nature's noblemen. Instead of serving as a contradiction to prevailing theories, Job's obvious civilized and educated traits were overlooked by influential philosopher-scientists of the slave era, cited in Chapter 1, who preferred to believe that there was no "civilization" in Africa. Further, his as-told-to-Bluett account of the experiences, feelings, and observations of an African transported into American slavery has not been considered representative of the experience of thousands of other Africans as discussed in American histories that tend to say there are no records of such matters. His memoirs do not appear in any collection of African American literature. This is a point I shall discuss later.

Job's full story has seldom been told, and the complete text of his book has seldom been reprinted. Perhaps because it is a proud affirmation of native African culture, religion, and family rather than an unsophisticated tale of the trials faced by a pitiable black person fleeing, alone, from cruel slaveholders and crushed slaves—the common fare of the once and again popular "slave narratives"—it has been underplayed where it might count. In addition, it has been overlooked when it might have provided a model, in part at least, for later African and African American memoirs or freedom narratives.

Job's life story is dramatic, ironic, and informative; so is his book. Its hero is energetic; daring; clever; politic; and, like most real people, less than perfect; its author, writing for Job, is well meaning in every sense of the term. The book's title was almost an outline: *Some MEMOIRS of the LIFE of JOB, the SON of SOLOMON the High Priest of Boonda in Africa; Who was a Slave about two Years in Maryland; and afterwards being brought to England, was set free, and sent to his native Land in the Year 1734.* On the title page, the amanuensis author identifies himself as "THOMAS BLUETT, Gent. who was Intimately acquainted with him [Job] in America, and came over to England with him." Its obligatory flattering dedication to the Duke of Montague declares that Job "requested me to write an Account of him, and to lay the same before YOU, as an Acknowledgment of your GRACE's great Humanity and Goodness to an unfortunate Stranger." Bluett added that he hoped that his having "not been us'd to such Matters as these" would pardon any literary shortcomings. He also wanted to be pardoned for any factual errors: "The Facts I have inserted, are what I had by JOB's particular information, or from my own Knowledge." Bluett insisted on this last point at length in an introduction to *Some Memoirs*; he intended "to advance nothing as Fact, but what I either knew to be such, or have had from JOB's own Mouth, whose Veracity I have no reason to doubt of."

Bluett's Section 1 offers "An Account of the Family of JOB; his Education; and the more remarkable Circumstances of his Life, before he was taken Captive." Job had been a freeman in a respectable community. Job's African name was Hyuba (Ayuba), boon Salumena, boon Hibrahema (Ibrahima), hence anglicized as Job, the son of Solomon, the son of Abraham, of the major Fulbe clan of Jallo. He said he was about thirty-one or thirty-two, which places his birth around 1702. His country's boundaries were unclear to Bluett and perhaps to Job, whose people did not mark off territory as the English did, and in fact the history of Bundu, the easternmost region of present-day Senegal, involves complicated territorial changes related to the rise and fall of princes and powers.

What is known of his country's history today is close to that given by Bluett: that a settlement was organized about fifty years earlier as a safety zone for every Muslim (all who could "read and know God") fleeing slavery. Job's family filled religious offices (*alfa*), and Job had been expected to do the same. He studied under his father, who had another student whom Job says became king. In fact, this Samba Geladio Jegi never got to be king but did become the subject of several epic song cycles still sung today. When Job was fifteen years old, he assisted his father as *imam*. At about the same age, he married the daughter of the Alfa of Tombut (Bambuk—gold country). They had three sons: Abdullah, Ibrahim, and Samba. He married a second wife around 1729, the daughter of the Alfa of Tomga (Damga), who gave him a daughter. Obviously, Job was doing well in Bundu. But he did himself little good when he set off on a trading venture toward the Atlantic Ocean, some two hundred miles from home.

Bluett's Section 2 offers the tale "Of the Manner of his being taken Captive; and what followed upon it, till his Return." This "slave narrative" section takes up only one and a half pages out of fifty-four. Job, with two servants, was sent to the distant Gambia River by his father to sell "two Negroes" (probably not Muslim and not Fulbe) and to buy paper and other items from an English ship; his father warned him against crossing the river into enemy Mandingo territory. Such trading ventures to dispose of criminals or enemies were not uncommon.

But Job seems to have had his own mind. He disagreed with Captain Pike's price for the two men; sent two personal servants home; engaged a translator, Loumein Yoai (Lamine Jay), and crossed the river. There he traded his two captives for some cows. While he was resting, having removed his "Gold hilted Sword, a Gold Knife, which they wear by their Side, and a rich Quiver of Arrows," seven or eight men took him and Jay captive. Their heads were shaved so they would appear to be prisoners of war, and they were then sold to the same Captain Pike to whom Job had tried to sell other men only days earlier. Pike allowed Job to try to get friends to ransom him, but a week passed, and Job and Jay were then taken across the sea to Annapolis, Maryland. (Exactly the same journey was made in 1750 by Kunta Kinte, Alex Haley's farthest-back ancestor in his novel and teleplay *Roots*.) Later Job heard that his father had sent slaves to be traded for Job and that his friend Samba had made a successful war on the Mandingoes, but they were too late to help Job.

The slaving agent in Annapolis, Vachell Denton, sold Job to a Mr. Tolsey in Kent Island, Maryland, who put him to work preparing tobacco for market. Job malingered and was sent to take care of cattle—a task that a Fula would have been pleased to have. However, Job's unhappiness and his faith led to much praying. At least once a white boy threw mud in his face as Job prostrated himself in the manner of Muslims everywhere. Job ran away in hopes of finding a better master or situation. Getting as far as southeastern Pennsylvania, he was taken up by the local sheriff, as both black and white servants were who could not prove that they were free or unindentured, if they had no pass and no excuse for being where they were. Job was put in prison.

Bluett and others, having heard something of Job, visited him in June 1731. They discovered Job could speak no English, but they encouraged the affable, calm man to write if he could. He wrote, pronounced the words "Allah" and "Muhammad," and refused wine, so they concluded that Job was a Muslim. Bluett and others called him a "Mahometan," a term that Muslims, including Job, find offensive because it suggests worship of a man rather than of God or

Allah. It appears that Job's objection was not understood by Bluett. No one at that time knew what to do about Job.

A slave who could speak Wolof, a language of Senegal that Job understood, discovered who Job's master was and what Job's problems with him were. The jailer returned Job and explained that Job thought he deserved to be treated better. As a result, Job was given a place to pray. But he was not reconciled to being a slave and wrote a letter in Arabic to his father. He had it taken to the man who had received him in Annapolis, who eventually got it to England. On the way, however, the philanthropist James Oglethorpe—founder, in the originally antislavery colony of Georgia, of an asylum for many British people who were imprisoned victims of a court system as arbitrary as some in Africa saw the letter and helped arrange a bond to release Job on a promise to pay his happy-to-sell master.

Several Annapolis gentlemen (ministers and lawyers) helped take care of Job, were taught some Arabic, and recommended him to London friends for his good nature and obvious spirituality. They might have recommended him for his Muslim faith, had it occurred to them, because that was what was clearly sustaining him. Finally, in March 1733, Job and Bluett set sail for England. On this passage, Job impressed Bluett and others by writing out the Quran from memory; by his religious devotion, praying publicly five times a day; his adherence to Muslim dietary rules; and by his pleasant way with the officers and crew. Bluett and the captain took it upon themselves to teach Job English. In about twenty days he had learned to write single syllables. Then Job and Bluett both became ill, but by the time another month had passed and they had arrived in England, Job was able to take part in common conversations.

For some time this Muslim pilgrim's progress was threatened; Job was still property, though in England. Bluett had become his friend and, as a lawyer, strove to make Job comfortable and his freedom secure through several useful contacts. Job was eventually introduced to a number of powerful people who were sympathetic to his cause. But a high price had been set on Job, and for a while it appeared that a proposed subscription might not raise enough to buy his freedom. Eventually the Royal African Company, Job's owner at the time, was paid and began preparations for sending Job back to the Gambia. Job was relieved to hear that there would be no ransom to pay once he arrived.

Already Job had gained extraordinary encouragement and treatment above nearly everyone's expectations. Job's impressive ways brought him invitations, friendships, and gifts through a period of more than a year in England. The man was busy. Significant intellectual and political gentry took him in; he met the royal family, his curiosity about and ability to handle agricultural and other tools led to gifts worth more than five hundred English pounds, and he gathered more money and enough other valuables to make his return to the Gambia luxurious by any standards. Further, along his way Job politely disputed with Christian divines; wrote three Qurans from memory; and translated Arabic for Sir Hans Sloane (one of the founders of the British Museum) and others, probably including George Sale, whose translation of the Quran in English in 1734 was hailed as the best to date. (Job sent greetings to someone his English secretary called "Mista Sail" in a letter written from the Gambia in 1736. It is possible that he contributed something to that translation.) Job was also elected to the prestigious and intellectual Spalding Gentlemen's Society, which may have put him in the company of philosopher-physicist Sir Isaac Newton and poet Alexander Pope.

Bluett's Section 3, "Some Observations, as related by JOB, concerning the Manners and Opinions of his Countrymen," gives further hints about the man and the culture that so impressed the English nobility. Bluett began by reiterating the prevailing opinion of his day on the generally "hard and low life" of most Africans because of the lack of European conveniences. His description of African farming, milling, transportation, and construction by the laboring classes is grim; his sympathies for members of the higher classes having to read without candles in dark, hot houses is touching. But Bluett felt better because nearly every helpful item Job's people might need was sent along with Job.

Bluett was wonderfully ignorant of Africa. He was gullible too, of course. But his retelling, to give him due credit, is not the usual series of negative pictures. Indeed, it is quite romantic and refined in an expected Anglocentric way. Bluett passed on stories from Job about lions and elephants that he may or may not have misheard. He was fascinated by Job's descriptions of poisoned arrows used in hunting—as were other Englishmen who pestered Job for samples after his return to the Gambia. Job also described Fulbe customs of courtship, dowries, marriage, multiple wives, and divorce. Bluett does seem to have completely misunderstood the wives' wearing of the veil as being constant in the house as well as out. The naming of children on the seventh day, a kind of baptism, and circumcision are mentioned, as are prayers for the relatives of the dead. Here too Bluett seems to have tried to respect and to report honestly, though he barely understood what he was told about these customs.

Undoubtedly Job had impressed Bluett with the idea that such facts were to be emphasized in his book and seems also to have insisted on passing on his deeper observations. Accordingly, Bluett began in this section to try to characterize Job's religion. Bluett thought Job's religious thinking was less gross and material than what he had heard from Turks; he also felt Job's aversion to images was an improvement over Catholic ways.

Bluett's Section 4, "Of JOB's Person and Character," is more interesting because it is more detailed. We begin to see the man, if not the African, that Bluett and other English people saw: "JOB was about five Feet ten Inches high, straight limb'd, and naturally of a good Constitution; altho' the religious Abstinence which he observed, and the Fatigues he lately underwent, made him appear something lean and weakly. His Countenance was exceeding pleasant, yet grave and composed; his Hair long, black, and curled, being very different from that of the Negroes commonly brought from Africa." Notice there is no mention of his color. The same kind of de-Africanizing happened to others described later in this book.

Job had often been ingenious in conversation, showing a "solid judgment, a ready memory, and a clear head." He had also been able to argue his own religious principles with "much Temper and Impartiality," wit, "innocent simplicity"—which seems to have meant, to Bluett, the opposite of duplicity— and agreeably entertaining honesty. And he was able to do so in his only recently learned English. Job surprised many when he quickly took apart and put together several "ordinary instruments" (a plow, a grist mill, and a clock). And, Bluett says, he often wrote in Arabic—the Quran, for instance. No copies of these writings have yet been discovered, although a Quran was reported to be in the hands of a Mr. Smith around 1800. Letters from Job that have been discovered, written after his return to Africa, have not been impressive; that is, none of those extant reveals a facility beyond basic Arabic—the accompanying texts are not translations. Job may have decided that it mattered little what he wrote in Arabic because the rest of the page included his dictation in English. And who could read the Arabic, anyway?

Job appeared to everyone, Bluett thought, to be mild-tempered, compassionate toward the distressed, cheerful, never irreligious, and unfailingly wellmannered. Fearing, perhaps that this picture might make his man out to be a wimp, he added that he thought Job could also be brave, citing Job's tale of fighting robbers in Africa who attempted but failed to take away four "Negroes" Job was trying to sell. Further, regarding his religion, Job relaxed in one area: he modified his opposition to having a portrait of himself made as a remembrance for his English friends. But he did not yield on another. After reading carefully in the New Testament (in Arabic) he could not find anything about the Trinity, or three gods, that Christians worshipped. He found no reason to change his ideas in that regard. Bluett, a Christian missionary, conceded that though a Muslim, Job held "just and reasonable" beliefs about God and the next life.

Finally, Bluett decided that Job was quite learned despite the latter's referring to the existence of only thirty handwritten manuscripts as texts he had studied in his education; added his own misunderstandings of Job's discussions of the original transcription of the Quran and of how Arabic was taught; and gave Job's conclusion that Job respected Jesus Christ but that Muhammad had had to perfect the earlier prophet's message.

Of course, Bluett had to elevate Job above other Africans that the Royal African Company was exporting to America. Most later readers followed his lead, to the further detriment of images of Africans.

Bluett's "CONCLUSION; Containing some Reflections upon the Whole" reaffirms his belief that the providence of God—including Job's—shone brightly in the case of Job and that his trials, followed by the hospitality and kindness to strangers of good Englishmen—as well as their helpful gifts— would ultimately be beneficial to Job's countrymen. Then he let himself go: "Considering the singular Obligations he is under to the English, [Job] may possibly, in good time, be of considerable Service to us also; and that we have reason to hope this, from the repeated Assurances we had from JOB, that he would, upon all occasions, use his best Endeavours to promote the English Trade before any other."

This passage reveals a side of Bluett and a rationale for his pamphlet that were not admitted earlier. Instead of presenting Job as an example or representative of countless Africans with intellectual and spiritual acquirements and qualities that should have discouraged trading in their bodies and encouraged developing humane relations, Bluett represented Job as being nearly an English gentleman in mind, manners, religion, and love for things English—especially commerce and profits.

Job would probably have approved of the commercial promise anticipated by Bluett. He might also have liked to read or hear about how well he had negotiated his release, invitations to high places, and the charitable tendencies he cultivated so well. But he surely would have wanted his amanuensis to express more respect for his culture and people, Muslims generally, and their right to be as free as the English were. As we shall see later, Job acted immediately on the opening his reception in England had made.

Nonetheless, in his "Conclusion" Bluett introduced a warning deeper perhaps than he knew, and one that Hume, Kant, Hegel, Jefferson, Webster, and their followers should have taken to heart and head: "'Tis true, neither the Extent of our Lives nor Capacities will permit us to view any very great Part of the Works of God; and what we do see, we are too apt to put a wrong Construction upon."

Surely, in this conclusion, Bluett pronounced a profound warning to all those philosophers and others who dared offer opinions on that "Part of the Works of God" called Africans, despite never having visited or conversed with any of them. In *Some Memoirs* there was ample evidence that this representative African displayed a rational and critical intelligence, wit, self-consciousness, self-respect, apprehension of a godhead, debating skills, and manners—learned in his homeland and among fellow Muslims—to contradict such benighted Western theories. Had *Some Memoirs* been given the attention it deserved, it might have also been recognized as the first text in African American literature; been reprinted regularly; and provided a conceptual model, in part at least, for overlooked aspects of later African and African American memoirs or narratives.

But let us finish Job's post-Bluett story. Job's return voyage to Africa, a seven-week trip, was smoothed considerably by a very helpful letter dated July 4, 1734, signed by twelve officers of the RAC, and directed to the "Chief Merchants" in the Gambia. In it the RAC recommended good treatment for Job, requested care in returning him and his property to his own country, and described an agreement between him and the RAC that any Muslim sent as a slave to its agents should be freed upon offering two good non-Muslim slaves in exchange. Clearly Job had power—but clearly also, he had a lack of sympathy for those who had not accepted Islam.

This general letter was accompanied by a private letter emphasizing the company's interest in Job and saying the king and queen had also taken notice of him. It went on to urge the RAC officials in Africa to send someone with him to his own country in order to open "a trade and correspondence between the Nations of those parts and our highest factory" ("factory" being the RAC term for a trading post).

The most complete source of information on Job after he returned to Africa is Francis Moore, who was an RAC officer when Job was taken away and when he returned. Moore was as pleased with Job as any Englishman at home had been. He lived and traveled with Job for a year before leaving Africa for England in May 1735. He dedicated his *Travels into the Inland Parts of Africa . . . with a Particular Account of Job Ben Solomon . . .* to the Duke of Montague, a mutual acquaintance. Moore was one of the least racist of West African observers, and his *Travels* offers a clear picture of the Gambia people and Royal African Company operations. His book indicates that the Gambia trade at this time did not consist of slaves alone, although some captains, such as Pike, seemed to want nothing else. Moore strove to increase trade in ivory; gold; and gum, which had many industrial uses.

Moore's notes tell where Job and Lamine Jay were taken prisoner on the south shore of the Gambia River before being dragged off to Captain Pike. They also date Job's return as August 8, 1734. Moore appreciated Job's extraordinary good luck and politically astute progress from Annapolis through England and the gifts Job received from "her most Gracious Majesty Queen Caroline, his Highness the Duke of Cumberland, his Grace the Duke of Montague, the Earl of Pembroke, several Ladies of Quality, Mr Holden, and the Royal African Company."

Often during the rainy season they first shared, there were exciting moments. On August 26, Moore said he and his friend Job were peacefully sitting upriver when "there came by us six or seven of the very People who robb'd and made a slave of Job, about thirty Miles from hence, about three Years ago; Job, tho' a very even-temper'd Man at other times, could not contain himself when he saw them, but fell into a most terrible Passion, and was for killing them with his broad Sword and Pistols, which he always took care to have about him."

Moore claimed that he talked Job out of attacking them and persuaded him to ask questions of them instead. Job was delighted when he heard that a pistol received as part of the barter for Job had accidentally killed the king of the robbers' country.

Job sent messengers to Bundu; locals knew of only one other person sold to Europeans who had returned to Africa instead of being murdered or eaten as Africans often presumed was the fate of those taken away. Meanwhile, he talked and traded, prayed, gave away valuable sheets of paper, bought a woman slave and two horses, and waited to hear from home, about a week's journey away. The rainy season was not a good time to travel. There was another reason he had not heard anything: An intrafamily war was raging in a small country between the Gambia and Bundu.

Finally, however, early in February 1735, friends came from Bundu. They did not have good news. His respected father had died, although not until he had heard from Job, then in England. There had been a terrible war between rival factions, one of which included Job's fellow student Samba Geladio Jegi, and his first wife had remarried. Perhaps a bit doubtful about his African future, Job sent several letters with Moore, who was leaving Africa for England. In them Job promised to learn English and to increase English trade and influence while he remained in Africa. He also asked for help in finding and freeing Lamine Jay. In June Job managed to return to Bundu, where there had been doubts about the truth of Job's being free and relatively nearby. After a lively welcome-back party, Job and his dull English companion stayed in Bundu for five months, renewing old acquaintances and arranging trade.

Job had a few more adventures that were heard of in England. It was probably easy in those years traveling back and forth between Bundu and the Gambia. For a year Job was a prisoner or parolee of French powers trying to control the trade in gum and gold on either side of Bundu. The British were unable to protect Job, but his release was gained by Africans themselves when Muslim traders diverted all trade to the British on the Gambia River and away from the French on the Senegal.

From 1738 to 1740 little seems to have been heard from Job. In that last year Job requested passage to London, but gifts were sent instead. In 1750 the failing Royal African Company folded. Only a note in the prestigious Spalding Gentlemen's Society records suggests a continuing correspondence between one of its more distant members and Job, but it also indicated Job's death. Job Ben Solomon Jallo had died in 1773—the year Phillis Wheatley, who may have also come from Senegal, published her volume of poetry in London and Boston and three years before the Declaration of Independence blamed England for most colonial problems, including those related to the presence of African slaves in the New World.

The English undoubtedly had not gained all they wanted from this friendly investment, but they also seem not to have known how to use Job. It was a long time before they seriously financed another penetration into the African interior. Job, on the other hand, must have derived some advantages as well as some disappointments from his own hopes. But he too seems not to have known how best to use the English. It is possible, of course, that he could not bring himself to that pitch of purpose that might have been most useful to both, and it is also possible that his Muslim faith—almost forgotten in the RAC commercial records—allowed him to take the evil and the good as Allah willed. Whatever one concludes, this probably unexceptional small trader had shown for a short time and in a little space that at least one African was no "senseless, brutish" creature, whether in Maryland, England, or Bundu.

SELECTED READINGS

Stephen Belcher, "Constructing a Hero: Samba Geladio Djegui," *Research in African Literatures* 25 (Spring 1994), 75ff.

Philip D. Curtin, "Ayuba Suleiman Diallo of Bondu," in Philip D. Curtin, ed., *Africa Remembered: Narratives by West Africans from the Era of the Slave Trade* (Madison: University of Wisconsin Press, 1967).

Frances Smith Foster, *The Development of Ante-Bellum Slave Narratives* (Westport, Conn.: Greenwood, 1979).

Michael A. Gomez, *Pragmatism in the Age of Jihad: The PreColonial State of Bundu* (Cambridge: Cambridge University Press, 1992).

Douglas Grant, *The Fortunate Slave: An Illustration of African Slavery in the Early Eighteenth Century* (London: Oxford University Press, 1968).

Ronald A. T. Judy, *(Dis)Forming the American Canon: African-Arabic Slave Narratives and the Vernacular* (Minneapolis: University of Minnesota Press, 1993) 149–161.

Fig. 10. Ibrahim Abd ar-Rahman, Engraving of Crayon Drawing by Henry Inman, New York, 1828, from *The Colonizationist and Journal of Freedom*, Boston, 1834, frontispiece, photo courtesy of Amherst College.

4

Abd ar-Rahman and His
Two Amazing American Journeys

The year 1828 must have been an exciting one for both the dignified slave "Prince," of Natchez, Mississippi, and the haughty warrior Ibrahim Abd ar-Rahman Jallo, formerly of Timbo, Futa Jallon, Guinea—for they were one and the same man. After forty years of slavery on the American frontier, the six-foot-tall, newly freed sixty-five-year-old was permitted to quit his exile and to begin to make a long way home with his American-born wife, Isabella. As we shall see, this journey was almost a triumphant march in regal costume with himself at the head. Few cities and few dignitaries missed seeing or hearing about the couple or the man. This amazing trip, conducted on steamboats and stage-coaches by way of Cincinnati to Washington, D.C., through three New England states, New York City, Philadelphia, Baltimore, and eventually by boat to Norfolk, Virginia, and then to Liberia, about three hundred miles from his African hometown and nearly six thousand miles from Natchez, took eleven months (April 8, 1828 to March 18, 1829).

How much shorter this voyage must have seemed to the old but digni-fied, brave man than his trip in the other direction at age twenty-six. At that earlier time, usually in chains, Abd ar-Rahman had been led to the Gambia River and put into the tight and filthy hold of a small slave ship, the *Africa,* which brought him to Dominica Island in the West Indies, from where he was transshipped to New Orleans and then sent by riverboat to Natchez—about six thousand miles altogether and six months of nearly constant imprisonment during which he was clad in little more than his skin (mid-March into August 1788). This detailed information—more than is available on the journeys of most Africans brought as slaves to the New World—has been discovered in the comprehensive statements made by ar-Rahman to numerous contemporaries and through the extraordinary efforts of historian Terry Alford, detailed in his book *Prince Among Slaves* (1977). My own investigations, more modest than Alford's, differ only in giving less emphasis to ar-Rahman's royal pretensions.

In 1828, Abd ar-Rahman was the most famous African in America. This fame was a result of an unusual and unusually publicized manumission that the United States government encouraged, leading to his proud passage through many Northern cities in what a Mississippi sponsor thought was a Moorish costume: white turban topped with a crescent, blue cloth coat with yellow buttons, white pantaloons gathered at the ankles, yellow boots—and, sometimes, a scimitar! It was also a result of an extraordinary combination of the admiration and assistance of powerful and influential and not so powerful people—black and white—with widely varying agendas, as well as ar-Rahman's proud but politic words and faith-inspiring demeanor.

Abd ar-Rahman made positive impressions everywhere he went, despite the fact that he was begging for money to buy his children out of slavery. Each of those who helped him—several doing so despite prior prejudices against blacks and Muslims—was impressed by the man's modesty, persistence, and patience. They were also impressed by his history. As he told them, he had been, after all, a Muslim who believed in one god; a prince; an African able to read and write; a cavalry officer; a husband and father back home before suffering an unexpected defeat in war; a captive on the water until he was landed in Natchez; a runaway and then a steady, serious worker and family man, a model to other slaves, according to all local accounts; and finally a freeman wanting to save his whole family. Everyone who met him and left a record—and these were many—made admiring statements.

In that year of 1828, ar-Rahman saw much of the Northeast by way of invitations to influential homes and assembly halls in Washington; Baltimore; Philadelphia; New York City; Boston; Worcester, Salem, New Bedford, and Springfield in Massachusetts; Providence, Rhode Island; New Haven and Hartford, Connecticut; and smaller towns along the way. His seriousness and literacy led prominent white mercantile, philanthropic, and political people, including businessmen Charles and Arthur Tappan; colonizationists Francis Scott Key and Ralph R. Gurley; Rev. Thomas Gallaudet, founder of the first, school for deaf-mutes; Mayor Joseph Watson of Philadelphia; U.S. Representative Edward Everett, Jr.; Secretary of State Henry Clay; and a helpful but, as usual, reserved President John Quincy Adams, to positively respond in some way. African American leaders responded the same way, in Boston—including David Walker, who would soon fire the first meaningful shot in the war against American slavery with his bold *Appeal . . . To the Colored Citizens of the World* (1829); New York—including the two editors of the first black newspaper in America, *Freedom's Journal,* one of whom, John Russwurm (Bowdoin 1827) would follow ar-Rahman to Africa; and Philadelphia. The general public and the artist Henry Inman, who limned ar-Rahman's "quite black" features for posterity, were also touched. Forty years later, Inman's crayon portrait elicited a particularly unguarded reaction from a less than comic Mark Twain mentioned earlier, which I will return to later in this chapter.

Furthermore, "Prince's" progress, at least from the time he arrived in Cincinnati on April 19, 1828, to the time he left for Liberia on February 7, 1829, was described fully by the Northern press, which emphasized his attempts to raise money to ransom his children and grandchildren still enslaved near Natchez. His ten-month passage was also described by a segment of the Southern press, but fearfully, even insanely, as it claimed that the "red-eyed" freeman was inspiring anti-Southern, antislavery sentiments in the North and bloody insurrection in the South. More on this later.

Sometime lawyer Cyrus Griffin, who had helped free ar-Rahman, probably had been, a year earlier, the only Southern newspaper editor to publish four biographical articles on a single slave—ar-Rahman, of course. Griffin apparently thought he had to make the literate African into something more presentable, so he titled his series "The Unfortunate Moor." To make that misrepresentation more reasonable, he argued that the man had been lighter skinned when he came to America and that his hair had grown woolly only as it had grown whiter. The very man who was most responsible for his freedom, another editor, Andrew Marschalk, later became one of ar-Rahman's sudden Southern enemies on the grounds that those who encouraged his lengthy campaign were acting contrary to the condition Abd ar-Rahman's master had set on his being freed, that he "should only enjoy liberty in his native country." That is, that the couple was to have been sent immediately to Africa. This condition did exist, but Marschalk had known that a year earlier when he was among those who encouraged ar-Rahman to ask for help in buying his children.

Through it all—not aware, of course, of the vicious extremes reached by some Southern newspaper attacks—the elderly African kept his composure.

Though with what must have been wonder-inspiring vistas and close-ups of the most populous, busy, and technologically advanced part of the then youthful United States and almost constantly a focus of variously motivated personal attention, ar-Rahman did not become distracted or befuddled. In hopes of helping his family, he promised ministers he would preach Christianity, promised merchants he would promote trade, and showed promise of being very helpful to the American Colonization Society (ACS) in its goal of exporting black freed people to Liberia. Yet to his great credit, despite all these uses whites wanted to make of him, he also joined the ACS's African American opposition not just once but in galas arranged in three of the major cities named earlier.

Abd ar-Rahman was, to a great extent, personally successful. He and his wife did get to Liberia, and a year later the $3,500 he had raised in the Northeast was used to purchase the freedom and passage to Africa of eight of his descendants. That he seemed to have done little to advance Christianity or trade, having openly reverted to Islam immediately upon his ship's dropping anchor and having been at odds with the colony's manager, undoubtedly did not indicate a lack of success to him. But surely he must have been less than happy when the negotiations for the release of his children dragged on and when, later, he felt too ill to make the fifteen-day journey from Monrovia, the capital of Liberia, home to Timbo in the mountainous Futa Jallon. Whatever his feelings were, death ended them less than five months after he had returned to the Old World, and ar-Rahman did not get to see either his American children or his African homeland again.

This brief outline of Abd ar-Rahman's last two years barely suggests how interesting, valuable, and dramatic his full story is. There are numerous contemporary documents from friends and foes: dozens of newspaper articles and personal letters, U.S. government papers, a biographical pamphlet, and at least five manuscripts in Arabic by Abd ar-Rahman. Nearly all of these documents appear in my book *African Muslims in Antebellum America: A Sourcebook*.

There have been several retellings of his story, and, recently, growing attention to his particular adventures. As well as Alford's 1977 book, mentioned earlier, ar-Rahman was the subject of "The Biography of a Slave" by Charles Sydnor (1937); a few pages in *The African Colonization Movement, 1811–1865* by P. J. Staudenraus (1961); a book-length, romantic, and racist life story with possible folkloric value, James Register's *Jallon: Arabic Prince of Old Natchez* [1968]); and some short biographical and autobiographical statements have been reprinted elsewhere. The essential records had been available for some time, of course, but they appeared together in my previous book for the first time. Many come from that last year of ar-Rahman's life, but several of these and other documents refer to his earlier years on either side of the Atlantic.

The reasons for this man's remarkable self-possession may be presumed from his African history. He claimed to be the son of a Fula, the second *almaamy* (or religious and military leader) in the Futa Jallon region of present-day Guinea. His father was Ibrahima Yoro Pate Sori of the Jallo clan. He was eventually called Maudo, or the Great, because he was chiefly responsible for the success of a Fulbe-led series of wars of liberation and conquest against local non-Muslims that began in the late 1720s. Traditional stories abound concerning this earliest and most influential West African Fulbe *jihad* and its two leaders, the orthodoxly religious Karamoko Alfa and the warlike and commercially oriented Ibrahima Sori. As these legends do not differ much the main outlines of the history of eighteenth- and early nineteenth-century Futa Jallon are also easy to come by.

Abd ar-Rahman's more particular place in Futa Jallon, as is to be expected of a man who disappeared in his midtwenties, is not readily discoverable. But there is sufficient information in his autobiographical statements relative to what is known about his country's history to offer the following sketch.

Abd ar-Rahman was born around 1762 and was well educated in centers of Islamic training—at home in Timbo, where Bilali also hailed from (see Chapter 5); in Jenne of Masina, the home of Salih Bilali (see Chapter 5); and in Timbuktu, birthplace of Abu Bakr (see Chapter 2)—cities and areas that witnessed Fulbe-led *jihads* in the early nineteenth century. Ar-Rahman was not an Arab or Moor, as several reporters claimed; he was "quite dark" and had curly hair and African features, as Inman's portrait shows. He did cherish a Fulbe sense of superiority to all other people, black and white—a sentiment reduced to anti-Africanism by earlier writers. Not being a first son—hence not especially assigned to advanced intellectual pursuits—he assumed military training and duties. His father needed all the help he could get. From long before ar-Rahman's birth, the Fulbe and their sometime allies had been constantly at war, usually on the defensive. Finally, however, in years that would be similarly significant in North America, 1776 to 1778, Sori managed to consolidate his then victorious armies and power and to create not only the strongest nation of its time in that area but a safe haven for some of the most influential Islamic scholars in West Africa. With a basis in trade and agriculture, including capturing, utilizing, and selling slaves, this political and economic empire was closely related to the Atlantic trade in Africans.

By the time Abd ar-Rahman was twenty-two, literate in Arabic and able to speak the Bambara, Mandingo, and Jallonke languages, at the very least, he had already seen a large part of West Africa and its people and had successfully led sizable military forces. Four years later, in 1788, more experienced militarily, married, and a father, ar-Rahman led an army of two thousand west—in defense, he said, of his country's trade with Europeans on the coast. This trade included exporting enemies during the years of the *jihad,* which had both religious and political ends, and later outright captures and sales of non-Muslims into the Atlantic slave trade because Europeans were not interested in any other items, according to ar-Rahman's half-brother, ruler Abdul Qadiri, in 1821. Altogether, in this expedition ar-Rahman would cover more ground than he would later traverse in his trip from Natchez to Boston. As he set out, he had no way of knowing that someday he would also be in a position to compare two quite different Atlantic-bound overland journeys and overseas voyages.

In this last of his African wars, he and his army of more or less recent converts were immediately successful. Since they could not capture the enemy's soldiers, however, they retired after inflicting what punishment they could. On the way home, the will of Allah turned against him. The prince and his cavalry troop were ambushed in a narrow mountain pass, and he and about fifty of his men were captured by the regrouped enemy called by Abd ar-Rahman the Houbous or Hebos, probably non-Muslims or lukewarm Muslims but not as yet identified beyond question. The captives were taken to the very distant Gambia River, where ar-Rahman was not able to find fellow Muslims to ransom him as was often done. Surely already sick in heart and spirit, he was sold to the captain of a waiting British ship. Ar-Rahman's long life in foreign slavery was about to begin.

As his modern biographer, Terry Alford, discovered, ar-Rahman experienced enough hardship for one lifetime before he was able to rest on land again. For half a year he was almost continually shipbound. He rode the Gambia River for a week; suffered the three-thousand-mile, six-week sail across the Atlantic to Dominica in the Caribbean; and then had to undergo another 2,200 miles and six more weeks' passage across the Caribbean to the Mississippi River. There he remained shipbound for another week before landing in Spanish New Orleans, a city then only two-thirds the size of Timbo. His waterborne ordeal was not yet over. After a month's stay there, he was finally carried three hundred miles upriver, and in another thirty days he had arrived at what was to be his home away from home, Natchez.

It is a wonder anyone survived such a journey. But ar-Rahman had been a warrior; survive he did. Ill, weak, and wrapped with rope, he was sold, shorn of his long hair, and named—by his purchaser, Thomas Foster—"Prince" because of his still proud ways and his attempt to tell of his African position through a Mandingo translator. Abd ar-Rahman, born to command and trained to despise agricultural labor, suffered whippings and field work, bided his time, grew well, and ran away. After some weeks in the woods of what was then Spanish Mississippi, however, he returned, disheartened, perhaps, in not discovering companies of fugitives he cared to join. In fact, a fellow Fula and Muslim had been sold with him, and he did meet others around Natchez. But they arranged no action together, as far as we know. Rahman became resigned to his fate and showed it in his behavior. His mistress, to whom he first reappeared, attributed his new attitude to the "power of [her] smile and [her] touch." The runaway may have been desperate for a human relationship of any kind, but it is more likely that he hoped that faithful service might be repaid with fair treatment, his own house, fields, free time, and some private life. Such was the treatment loyal slaves of the Fulbe received in Futa Jallon.

Within unavoidable bounds, Abd ar-Rahman distinguished himself further. The former commander became an overseer in practice, if not in name. Perhaps, too, as any Fula of his class would—particularly a cavalryman like him—he found familiar pleasures in caring for the horses and the cattle that his master bought regularly as time passed. He apparently strove to impress. His master declared that he had never known Abd ar-Rahman to be intoxicated, dishonest, mean, or lazy; fellow slaves and neighbors had few or no complaints against him. Abd ar-Rahman tried a show of conversion to the religion of his master and a show of disidentifying with the majority of American slaves. But he was not given his freedom in his prime years. His "marriage" to an American-born, and dark-skinned, Baptist in 1794 or 1795—a contradiction of his supposed religious and racial stance—was a personal success. And his daily life eventually became easier as he did finally get his own garden plot and release time.

In the midst of that struggle he had high and then dashed hopes. One day, perhaps in 1807, a very unlikely and nearly providential meeting took place. "Prince," relieved of some field duties, was selling vegetables his family had grown in Natchez town when he was seen by and reintroduced to the only white man ever to have resided in Timbo before or during his father's rule there in the early 1780s. John Coates Cox had wandered away from a ship on the coast of Africa, had grown terribly ill, and had eventually ended up in Timbo. After being restored to health and given a guard to the Gambia River by Abd ar-Rahman's father, he came to America and eventually emigrated to the

Mississippi territory. Cox and the vegetable seller recognized each other at once. Cox notified the governor and tried to arrange for the purchase and free-ing of the man he had known on such different terms nearly thirty years earli-er. But Foster would not sell ar-Rahman, and Cox's, and later his son's, attempts to buy him were unsuccessful.

Still, it is probable that Abd ar-Rahman became something of a local celebrity because of Cox's story and efforts on his behalf. Not long thereafter, ar-Rahman, now a father of five sons and four daughters, was relieved of all field duty, and his greater leisure led to his becoming even better known. Sometime in the early 1820s, he spent enough time with a local newspaper editor, Andrew Marschalk, who was impressed with Abd ar-Rahman's literacy and knowledge of West Africa, for Marschalk to suggest that he might be able to send a letter to Africa in ar-Rahman's Arabic. For some reason, perhaps because he had not seen any Arabic writing for thirty years, ar-Rahman did not take up this suggestion until 1826. Two years after the State Department received this letter and involved itself in a lengthy correspondence with Morocco—the only African Muslim nation with which the department was familiar—followed by some relatively easy negotiations, Secretary of State Henry Clay (a colonizationist and slaveholder) wrote that the United States would pay for the transportation of the "Moor" (as he was presumed by Marschalk to be) to Washington, D.C., if his master were agreeable and would free him. On February 22, Foster agreed on condition that his former proper-ty would be sent out of the country.

Then arose another snag. Ar-Rahman did not want to go without his wife. At this point his master balked somewhat. Isabella was, after all, "the planta-tion's obstetrick practitioner and doctress." Eventually, however, he gave in and set a low price of $200 for her freedom. In twenty-four hours local citizens raised $293 by subscription; by mid-March she too was free. Editor Marschalk, responsible for the freed couple's passage to the nation's capital, provided an "Arabian" costume for the "Moor"; enjoyed the going-away party (but for the tearful separation of parents and children); and sent them off, via the Mississippi River, north to Cincinnati. He entertained vague—and dangerous—hopes that along the way Abd ar-Rahman might be able to raise money to redeem his children. He did not anticipate, however, that he himself (partially inspired by Master Foster's anger at his former slaves being at large in America) would soon be the leading critic of the fund-raising campaign waged by ar-Rahman in the distant Northern states.

For nearly a year Abd ar-Rahman—then in his mid-sixties—traveled backward toward home. His overland march was sometimes under the care of the federal government, with an official "pass" provided by Secretary Clay. He dictated a letter home about that sponsorship. His amanuensis seems to have tried to give the true flavor of his words. The letter is appreciative, politic, and includes a caution about adding to the costs of freeing his progeny:

My Dear Children,

I proceeded to this place to see the President and Mr. Clay; they both received me very kindly, and I expect from their expressions to me, that they will pay every attention to my business. In Baltimore the gentlemen took me in a carriage around the town, and shew me all the beauties thereof. In Washington I visited the President's house, but I found the President the best piece of furniture in the house.

My reception by Mr. Clay was very flattering to me; he invited me to partake of the hospitalities of his house, which I declined, telling him of my good treatment at Williamson's hotel.

My dear boys, Simeon and Prince, for God's sake dont let Lee get a wife until you hear from me.

Sometimes he traveled under the care of American Colonization Society members and sympathizers and sometimes under his own inclinations. It was he who proposed, on the basis of the scheme that freed his wife, to raise money by a subscription; it was he who, through some misrepresentation that he would preach Christianity back in Africa, lured into his service several very helpful advocates; and it was he who bravely accepted invitations proffered by relatively poor but free African Americans, who were usually opposed to colonization.

Although he was not used, or did not allow himself to be used, as Job Ben Solomon had been by British geographers and Arabicists, he often wrote in Arabic for those who asked. A Rev. John F. Shroeder in New York concluded that Abd ar-Rahman wrote "with correctness and fluency. . . . He has read and written for me a great deal of Arabic." Without seeing these manuscripts, it is not possible to say whether Shroeder was praising penmanship or a range of statements. To others who asked for examples of his Arabic, ar-Rahman offered his version of the Lord's Prayer, which would have been consistent with his ostensible project of spreading the gospel upon his hoped-for return to Africa with all his children. What he actually wrote, however, was the Fatiha—the introductory Surah of the Quran, or part of it—wholly consistent with the

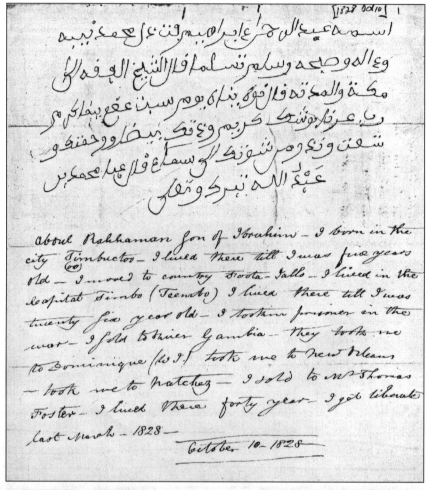

Fig. 11. Ibrahim Abd ar-Rahman, Variation on the Fatiha Presented as an Autobiographical Sketch and ar-Rahman's "Translation," October 10, 1828, from John Trumbull Papers, Yale University.

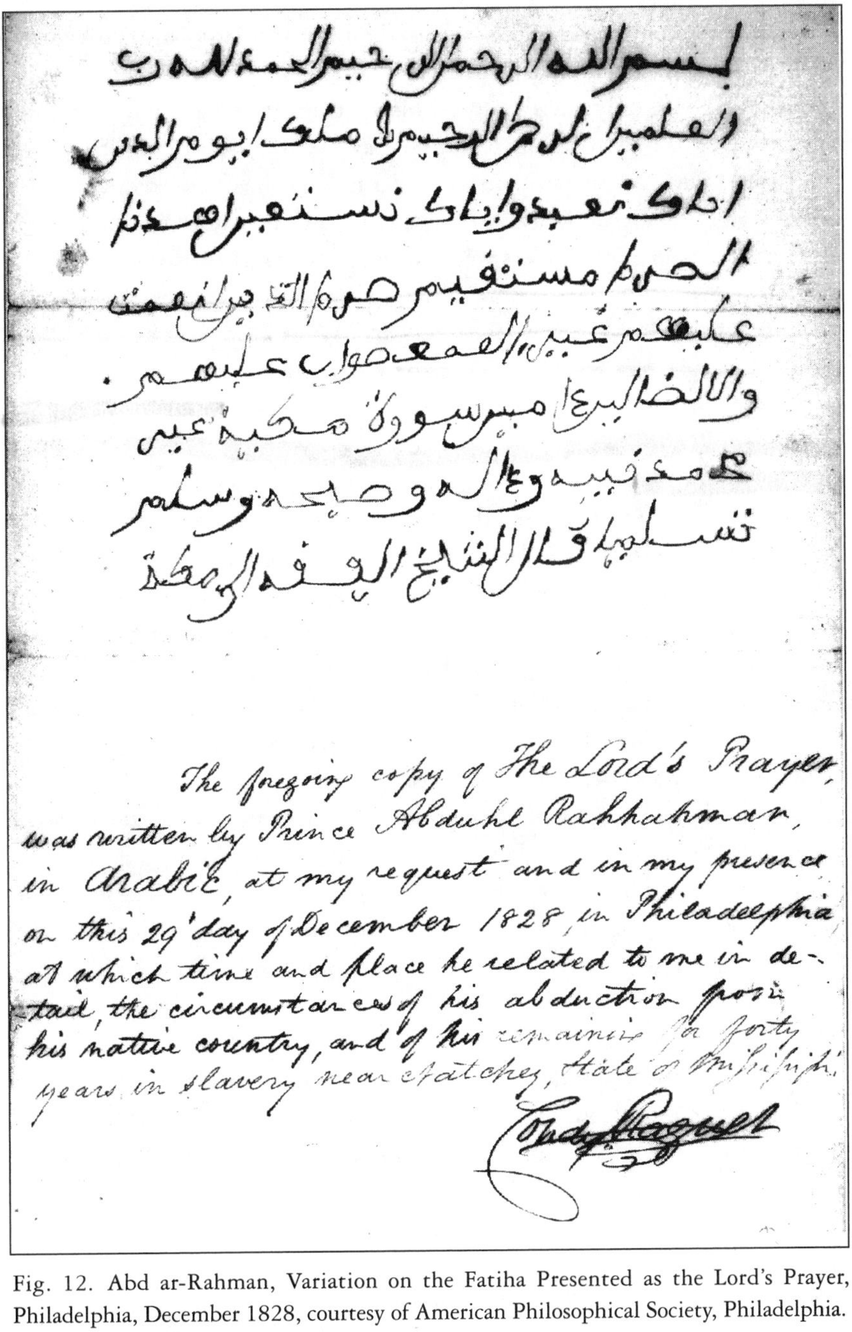

Fig. 12. Abd ar-Rahman, Variation on the Fatiha Presented as the Lord's Prayer, Philadelphia, December 1828, courtesy of American Philosophical Society, Philadelphia.

religion of his youth to which he was to return immediately upon re-viewing African soil and to which he had strictly adhered through 1828, according to Marschalk. Since only such scraps of his writings have been found so far, it appears possible that ar-Rahman may not have been capable of writing beyond the Fatiha. But what he wrote for Shroeder may yet be discovered. On another level, ar-Rahman must have been aware that greater exertions would not be recognized. Who of his readers would have known what he had written?

He had undoubtedly been uninterested in writing any Christian verses—even after being given a New Testament in Arabic. Abd ar-Rahman had not, after all, found Christianity to be perfect. He surely balked at believing in the Trinity and at any notion that Jesus was a final prophet. Muhammad enjoyed that special relationship to God in his cosmology. But ar-Rahman also offered specific criticisms. It was wrong that a man should be called good and a Christian even when he ignored the religion's essential precepts. He argued, "I tell you the Testament very good law; you no follow it; you no pray often enough; you greedy after money." "You good man; you join the religion." He paused, as if to better point out the incongruity. "See, you want more land, more neegurs; you make neegur work hard, make more cotton. . . . Where you find dat in your law?" In Futa Jallon's religion, law and economics were one. There, slave labor was different: "I tell you, man own slaves—he join the religion—be very good—he make he slaves work till noon—go to church—then till he sun go down they work for themselves—they raise cotton, sheep, cattle, plenty, plenty." His people's slaves were allowed lives of their own during parts of each day. A French visitor to Futa Jallon in 1817 said that Fulbe slave towns were "establishments truly honorable to humanity." Later visitors were less positive, but those captives who persisted in opposing the Fulbe were sent on to the coasts.

As he had done in the Old Southwest, ar-Rahman did what he had to do in the Northeast. He rode and walked for miles and sat through lengthy orations on colonization, on the spread of Christianity, and on the business opportunities he might originate. Throughout, he maintained the air and address of a prince as he told his story and suffered through long-winded rhetoric and well-meaning but ignorant declarations, such as, "He was a barbarian, and a slave; . . . man's victim, but nature's nobleman." He also seems to have remained his calm, dignified self when he marched and dined in a lively affair capped by some colorful toasts raised by Boston's black leaders. Abd ar-Rahman was also feted by blacks in New York's Abyssinian Baptist Church and in Philadelphia. In the former city he met the editor of the first African American newspaper, *Freedom's Journal*, who was very interested in his story. As noted earlier, John Russwurm followed him to Liberia. What Abd ar-Rahman thought about these occasions, unfortunately, has not been well recorded. There exists only his appreciative response to the toasts in Boston, and, by the way, a letter he wrote to try to talk Russwurm out of going to Liberia because he thought it would not be healthy for him.

Finally, on February 7, 1829, after having raised $3,500, Abd ar-Rahman and Isabella left on the first boat available to them, the *Harriet*, which carried 152 other emigrants—including Joseph J. Roberts, the future first president of Liberia. They brought an official passport signed by Clay and some supplies provided by the U.S. government. Thirty-seven days out of Norfolk, Virginia, land was sighted, and ar-Rahman was soon to find himself back in Africa. Although he had kept up with some of the history of his people by asking for information from recently arrived Africans in Mississippi and from Africans he had met in Hartford and New York City, he must have wondered what he would find. One brother, Almaamy Saadu (visited by an English exploring expedition in 1794), had been murdered in 1795; another, Almaamy Abdal, or Abdul Qadiri, who had been visited by British and French expeditions in 1816 and 1818, respectively, and again in 1821 by the British, had died in 1822 or 1825; and yet another brother, Almaamy Yah Ya, had been replaced in 1827 by a nephew who was to be ousted by a rival Alfaya family elder, Bubakr, that same year. This latter ruler was in power when René Caillié, the first European to enter and leave Timbuktu alive, and the slave trader Captain Theophilus Conneau visited Timbo and its environs in 1828.

As noted earlier, Abd ar-Rahman did not immediately push on to Timbo. The rains had to end, his health had to improve, and perhaps the news from home needed to be studied first. Besides, the fifteen-day journey up the mountain trails would be hard on a man his age. He corresponded with Timbo and America, and promises went back and forth between each. In late June, diarrhea and fever afflicted him. He left his manuscripts in the traditional Muslim way to teachers in Timbo before he died on July 6, 1829. Isabella remained to greet those of their children who were purchased only after the death in that presidential election year of ar-Rahman's former master who was rabidly pro–slave holding Andrew Jackson, violently anti-Adams, and now anti-"Prince." Eight of ar-Rahman's descendants arrived in Liberia in December 1830 and at least part of the family was free and reunited. It is possible that seven others, his son Prince and Prince's six children, got to Africa, but it is also possible that some children may have made the voyage in 1835, as a published report said that "William Foster [a brother of ar-Rahman's former owner] of Natchez, Miss., manumits by will, twenty slaves on condition of their going to Liberia, and bequests thirty dollars to each family."

Unfortunately, it is not known whether ar-Rahman's wife ever met any of her husband's African family, although one of her husband's countrymen hoped to bring her to Timbo. There is no indication either that Isabella or any of Abd ar-Rahman's offspring adopted his religion.

One part of this African's story has been bypassed in most retellings. The local newspaper editor who was most responsible for securing ar-Rahman's release, Andrew Marschalk, became embroiled in a heated newspaper war with several other editors, including Cyrus Griffin, who had given considerable publicity to "Prince" shortly after his departure for the North. Both men had been morally but not politically opposed to slavery, and both had had long and apparently satisfying conversations with ar-Rahman. Indeed, Griffin had published four articles in his Natchez newspaper on Abd ar-Rahman's history, homeland, and opinions. But the news of ar-Rahman's Northern travels and meetings and the several messages he sent to his family in Mississippi—acting and speaking as a free man and arousing, it was assumed, antislavery and anti-Southern sentiment, especially among blacks in Boston who seemed to be preaching slave solidarity and rebellion—led Griffin to fall silent and the paranoid and humorless Marschalk to declare that the freeman had become a weapon, political or worse, of the Clay-Adams party. His editorials prefigure the worst of the racist Democratic journalism of the post-Reconstruction era.

Marschalk reprinted the itinerary and toasts to Abd ar-Rahman in Boston and then published a series of inflammatory pro-Jackson articles declaring that President John Quincy Adams's spokesmen were "actually exciting the slaves to revolt, by the same species of arguments which produced the massacre of St. Domingo [Haiti, where all remaining whites were executed by Dessalines in 1804]." He also attacked and reattacked Griffin and even ar-Rahman as he tried to shake off his own responsibility in the latter's redemption. Newspapers from Natchez to New Orleans—and perhaps farther—reprinted some of these articles, or took sides for or against them, and were nearly as hysterical as Marschalk until Jackson's victory at the polls. At least one broadside for the Democrats offered an argument for voting the Jackson ticket that included references to Abd ar-Rahman.

Such emotionally primitive behavior and deliberate ignorance exemplified in this way and others by white Christians contrasted sharply with the impression created by the dignified African. Though apparently lacking in

some of the signs of the civilized man, ar-Rahman equally apparently exhibit-
ed the essentials. Congressman Edward Everett, Jr., who met ar-Rahman in a
committee room in the Capitol, later wrote an article in which he recognized
that "[some] Christians have not done much to recommend their faith." He
might also have added, "or their intelligence, particularly concerning Africans."
He had seen, on the other hand, admirable qualities—"strong sense . . . cultivated mind . . . calm courage, Christian [why not Muslim?] patience, and a
genial hope of better times"—in the African Muslim Abd ar-Rahman. Everett
recommended the depiction of such men in the newspapers of the day (1853)
as "lessons of encouragement" to fellow African Americans and as spurs to
doubts as to "whether there is that diversity of intellectual endowments between
the two races, which white men are too apt to take for granted."

The point—similar to a commentary on Lamine Kebe by his amanuensis
in 1835—was better presented than received, as the ethnographic, historical
and literary record shows. Influential scientific men such as Harvard's Louis
Agassiz were, in the 1850s, purveying theories of African inferiority not argued
earlier. Probably the least happy retelling of Abd ar-Rahman's American passage
is that by none other than Mark Twain, whose irrepressible cynicism about the
human—or male—species is matched by his irrepressible racism. The racist
attitudes that undermine the dignity of Jim in *Huckleberry Finn*, the depiction
of the varying fortunes of the twins—one black and one white—in *The Tragedy
of Pudd'nhead Wilson*, and the Mammy's honesty in "A True Story" also appear
in his response to the original of the engraving reproduced as the frontispiece
to this chapter. In 1867, in Hartford, Twain saw in Henry Inman's crayon
portrait a "dignified darkey of patriarchal aspect." But by the time he had
finished relating his host's, or his own, somewhat garbled understanding of ar-
Rahman's trials and return to Africa, Twain had reduced that image about as far
as he could: "I, for one, sincerely hope that after all his trials he is now peacefully enjoying the evening of his life and eating and relishing unsaleable niggers
from neighboring tribes who fall into his hands, and making a good thing out
of other niggers from neighboring tribes that are saleable."

Clearly this piece says more about the undignified Missourian in post–Civil
War America than about the dignified Muslim who, in fact, might have
indulged in slave trading but never in cannibalism. Fair retellings that did not
depict the literate Abd ar-Rahman as an Arab or a Moor or a monster and that
provided trustworthy sources had to wait for our own time.

A pattern was set as early as Cyrus Griffin's first letter (to the ACS,
December 1827) and four articles in his newspaper, the *Natchez Southern Galaxy*

(May 29, June 5 and 12, and July 5). The information came from ar-Rahman, and the letter and articles are informative. They tell a great deal about ar-Rahman's royal family, country, and religion; and show his intelligence and knowledge. But they are marred by Griffin's attempt to explain away ar-Rahman's dark skin, thick lips, and woolly hair as noted above. Griffin, a displaced New Englander, desperately wanted his literate friend to fit the title of "Moorish Prince," that is, to not be African.

I will close with a version of ar-Rahman's own tale. In Washington, D.C., Ralph R. Gurley, the indefatigable secretary of the ACS, was greatly impressed by the former slave. He had ar-Rahman write an autobiography in Arabic. It would be interesting to see this manuscript, but it has not yet been found. Ar-Rahman then translated it orally, and Gurley's transcription of this was printed in the society's journal, *The African Repository*, in May 1828 (77–81). Gurley prefaced this version as follows: "At our request, Prince has written a concise history of himself, and we have penned a translation of it from his own lips. The only liberty we have taken, is to correct those grammatical inaccuracies, which resulted from his imperfect knowledge of our language." Gurley clearly also polished at several points, but some of what must have been ar-Rahman's English comes through. It is a dramatic telling:

Abduhl Ar-Rahman's History

I was born in the City of Tombuctoo. My Father had been living in Tombuctoo, but removed to be King in Teembo, in Foota Jallo. His name was Almam Abrahim. I was five years old when my father carried me from Tombuctoo. I lived in Teembo, mostly, until I was twenty-one, and followed the horsemen. I was made Captain when I was twenty-one—after they put me to that, and found that I had a very good head, at twenty-four they made me Colonel. At the age of twenty-six, they sent me to fight the Hebohs, because they destroyed the vessels that came to the coast, and prevented our trade. When we fought, I defeated them. But they went back one hundred miles into the country, and hid themselves in the mountain.—We could not see them, and did not expect there was any enemy. When we got there, we dismounted and led our horses, until we were half way up the mountain. Then they fired upon us. We saw the smoke, we heard the guns, we saw the people drop down. I told every one to run until we reached the top of the hill, then to wait for each other until all came there, and we would fight them. After I had arrived at the summit, I could see no one except my guard. They followed us, and we ran and fought. I saw this would not do. I told every one to run who wished to do so. Every one who wished to run, fled. I said I will not run for an African [Kufr?]. I got down from my horse and sat down. One came behind and shot me in the shoulder. One came before and pointed his gun to shoot me, but seeing my clothes, (ornamented with gold,) he cried out, that! the King. Then every one turned down their guns, and came and took me. When they came to take me, I had a sword under me, but they did not see it. The first one that came, I sprang forward and killed. Then one came behind and knocked me down with a gun, and I fainted. They carried me to a pond of water, and dipped me in; after I came to myself they bound me. They pulled off my shoes, and made me go barefoot one hundred miles, and led my horse before me. After they took me to their own country, they kept me one week. As soon as my people got home, my father missed me. He raised a troop, and came after me; and as soon as the Hebohs knew he was coming, they carried me into the wilderness. After my father came and burnt the country, they carried me to the Mandingo country, on the Gambia. They sold me directly, with fifty others, to an English ship. They took me to the Island of Dominica. After that I was taken to New Orleans. Then they took me to Natchez, and Colonel F[oster] bought me. I have lived with Colonel F. 40 years. Thirty years I laboured hard. The last ten years I have been indulged a good deal. I have left five children behind, and eight grand children. I feel sad, to think of leaving my children behind me. I desire to go back to my own country again; but when I think of my children, it hurts my feelings. If I go to my own country, I cannot feel happy, if my children are left. I hope, by God's assistance, to recover them. Since I have been in Washington, I have found a good many friends. I hope they will treat me in other cities as they have treated me in the city of Washington, and then I shall get my children. I want to go to Baltimore, Philadelphia, and N. York, and then I shall return hither again.

His Interview With Dr. Cox

Dr. Cox was a surgeon on board a ship. He went ashore in Africa, and got lost. When he returned, he found the vessel gone. He set out to travel, and came into my country, Foota Jallo—our people saw him, and ran and told my father, that they saw a white man. My father told them to bring the white man here, that he might see him. They brought Dr. Cox, and my father asked him whither he was going. He said he knew not where to go, that the ship had left him, and that he had a bad sore leg. My father inquired what was the matter with his leg. He said he had wounded it in travelling. My father told him he had better go no farther, but stay with him, and he would get a woman to cure his leg. He was soon cured. My father told him to stay as long as he chose. He remained six months. One day my father asked him, if he wished to go to his own country. He said yes. My father said, what makes you desire to go back—you are treated well here? He answered, that his father and mother would be anxious, when the vessel returned without him, thinking he might be dead. My father told him, whenever you wish to go, I will send a guard to accompany you to the ship. Then fifteen men were sent with him by my father for a guard, and he gave him gold to pay his passage home. My father told the guard, that if a vessel was there, to leave the Doctor, but not to go on board the ship; and if there was no vessel, to bring the Doctor back. They waited some time, and then found the same vessel in which he came, and in that he took his passage. After that I was taken prisoner, and sent to Natchez. When I had been there sixteen years, Dr. Cox removed to Natchez, and one day I met him in the street. I said to a man who came with me from Africa, Sambo, that man rides like a white man I saw in my country. See when he comes by; if he opens but one eye, that is the same man. When he came up, hating to stop him without reason, I said master, you want to buy some potatoes? He asked, what potatoes have you? While he looked at the potatoes, I observed him carefully, and knew him, but he did not know me. He said boy, where did you come from? I said from Col. F's. He said, he did not raise you. Then he said, you came from Teembo? I answered, yes, sir. He said, your name Abduhl Ar-Rahman? I said, yes, sir. Then springing from his horse, he embraced me, and inquired how I came to this country? Then he said, dash down your potatoes and come to my house. I said I could not, but must take the potatoes home. He rode quickly, and called a negro woman to take the potatoes from my head. Then he sent for Gov. W[are]. to come and see me. When Gov. W came, Dr. Cox said, I have been to this boy's father's house, and they treated me as kindly as my own parents. He told the Gov., if any money would purchase me, he would buy me, and send me home. The next morning he inquired how much would purchase me, but my master was unwilling to sell me. He offered large sums for me, but they were refused. Then he said to master, if you cannot part with him, use him well. After Dr. Cox died, his son offered a great price for me.

Ar-Rahman knew how to make his points. After this exercise, the prince left for cities further north, and his strange story is history worth retelling in books or on the screen for general audiences.

SELECTED READINGS

Terry Alford, *Prince Among Slaves* (New York: Harcourt Brace Jovanovich, 1977).

For a version of the early rise of Futa (Fula) Jallon, see Jean Bayol, "Futa Jalon: Traditions of Jihad" (1882), in John D. Hargreaves, ed., *France and West Africa* (New York: St. Martin's Press, 1969), 111–113.

For information about Futa Jallon in the 1810s and 1820s, see Theophilus Conneau (also called Captain Canot). *A Slaver's Log Book, or 20 Year's Residence in Africa* (1854, rep.) (New York: Avon, 1976).

James Register, *Jallon: Arabic Prince of Old Natchez, 1788–1828* (Shreveport, La.: Mid-South Press, 1968).

P. J. Staudenraus, *The African Colonization Movement, 1811–1865* (New York: Columbia University Press, 1961).

Charles S. Sydnor, "The Biography of a Slave," *South Atlantic Quarterly,* XXXVI (January 1937), 59–73.

Mark Twain, "American Travel Letters, Series 2 [the last letter]," *Alta California,* August 1, 1869.

Fig. 13. Pages 11 and 10 of Bilali's Book, Sapelo Island, Georgia, c. 1840. Georgia State Library, Atlanta.

5

Bilali Mohammed and Salih Bilali: Almaamys on Georgia's Sapelo and St. Simon's Islands

Before the 1980s a few admiring contemporary references; an untranslated, mysterious manuscript in Arabic; a series of tales for children by the famous Joel Chandler Harris—creator of Uncle Remus—and a handful of remembrances by descendents in the 1930s gave Bilali of Sapelo Island, Georgia, a tiny space in the American cultural record. He should have been hard to miss because he regularly wore a fez and a long coat (as had Umar), he prayed facing the East on his carefully preserved prayer rug, and he always observed Muslim fasts and feast-day celebrations. When the time came, Bilali was buried with his rug and Quran. There was barely a hint, however, that the Fula from Timbo, Futa Jallon, compatriot and possible kin to Abd ar-Rahman, had been an *almaamy* (Fulfulde for Arabic *al-imam*), a leader of a Muslim community, or *umma,* within the antebellum United States.

Similar introductory notes may be made on his friend, fellow Fula Salih Bilali, called Tom, on St. Simon's Island—fifteen miles away in Georgia, but originally from Massina, Mali, nearly one thousand miles inland from Timbo. A few admiring contemporary references; an ethnography-biography in the form of a letter by his well-known master, James Hamilton Couper; and a handful of remembrances by descendants were, until recently, all the information to be found on this leader of another flock. Whether he too deserves the title *almaamy* is not absolutely settled.

Had extraordinary spiritual personalities and accomplishments in time of war and natural disasters inspired attention to slaves commensurate with that given to free whites, these two should have been famous Americans for their remarkable religious stories alone. The earliest notice includes no names but refers to both men. In a pamphlet published in 1829, an "enlightened" but roguish (he had at least two African wives—one who was a sort of queen in Florida and whose children did very well as they married whites in America), self-serving slaveholder and slave trader named Zephaniah Kingsley urged good treatment of slaves by masters and good treatment of such slave masters by other citizens of the world. Within the pamphlet's lengthy argument may be found his recollection of "two instances, to the southward, where gangs of negroes were prevented from deserting to the enemy [the British between 1812 and 1815] by drivers, or influential negroes, whose integrity to their masters and influence over the slaves prevented it; and what is still more remarkable, in both instances the influential negroes were Africans; and professors of the Mahomedan religion."

The second known mention appeared in Couper's almost admiring 1838 letter to his friend William Brown Hodgson, a student of North African languages and people, that was published by Hodgson six years later. Couper's subject is his black plantation driver-overseer Tom, or "Sali-Bul-ali." Toward the close, he mentions Salih Bilali's "intimate" Sapelo Island friend "Bul-ali." The letter says a great deal about Salih Bilali's homeland and history (some of which is repeated later in this chapter) but fails to mention the man's trials as a slave in America—a common omission in such writings.

Couper had a tradition to uphold. The wealthy, well-organized plantations of James Hamilton Couper, his father, John Couper, and Thomas Spalding of Sapelo Island were often visited by travelers. The most prominent were Aaron Burr shortly after his fatal duel with Alexander Hamilton; Basil and Margaret Hunter Hall from England, in 1828; John D. Legare, editor of the *Southern Agriculturist*, in 1832; Frances (Fanny) Kemble, famous British actress who married the *Gone With the Wind* Rhett-like Pierce Butler, in 1839; traveler-scientist Charles Lyell, another British traveler-scholar, who was interested in slave regimens and drivers like Salih Bilali, in 1846; Fredrika Bremer from Sweden, in 1851; and British courtier Amelia M. Murray, in 1855. All were convinced that their hosts were paragons of kindness and order as far as their slave people were concerned, although both Kemble and Bremer thought religious instruction for slaves was neglected and Kemble saw that too little was done to protect slave women from white overseers—especially on her husband's plantations.

Neither the masters, who wrote often for local journals, nor these visitors wrote about Bilali or Salih Bilali beyond Couper's letter and a somewhat confused note by Lyell. The latter was amused by the retention of some African names and appreciated that at least one slave (Salih Bilali) was intelligent and had a Muslim name, though Lyell insisted that the man's "jet-black children and grand children" had become Christians. Lyell added one other note: that during the War of 1812 (in 1815), Salih Bilali had persuaded about half of his slave people not to run off to waiting British ships whose officers had promised them freedom, by using the argument that he had lived under the British (in the Bahamas) and had not been pleased with his treatment there. As a matter of record, several took off anyway. Some ended up in Nova Scotia; a few seem to have been taken to Sierra Leone or Trinidad, where they served in British regiments and where some joined a Muslim Mandingo Society.

Bilali may have been more successful on Sapelo Island. He told Spalding that he could defend his charges, and Spalding's faith in his promises led him to give Bilali eighty muskets to defend the island property while his master was elsewhere. This appears to have been the only instance in which slaves were given guns in Georgia during the antebellum period. Bilali put his own faith on the line; he declared to Spalding that in the event of an attack, "I will answer for every Negro of the true faith, but not for the *Christian dogs* you own" (emphasis in original). Reportedly, no Spalding people fled to the British. However, at least one historian of the islands, Mary Bullard, told me that the British did not raid that far north.

In a second crisis, the terrible hurricane of September 1824, Bilali saved "hundreds of slaves" by directing them into cotton and sugar houses made of an African material called tabby (sand, lime, and oyster shells). There is no report of what happened on St. Simon's.

Except for a short note on Bilali and his family, who were met in the 1850s by Georgia Bryan Conrad, a resident of nearby Broughton Island ("They were tall and well-formed, with good features. . . . The head of the tribe was a very old man called Bi-la-li. He always wore a cap that resembled a Turkish fez" (from *Reminiscences of a Southern Woman*, c. 1901); a remark in an unpublished letter by Couper's son that Salih Bilali was the most religious man that he had ever known; and a reference in a history (Charles Spalding Wylly's *Seed . . . Sown in . . . Georgia*) from 1910, nothing was said about either man until the 1930s.

In 1933, the son of Francis Goulding, a popular children's writer who had befriended Bilali before the latter's death in 1859, willed a manuscript in Arabic that had been given to his father by Bilali to the Georgia State Library.

The son, an unreconstructed Southerner who averred that "Ben Ali"—as he decided to call him after reading books (discussed below) purportedly about Bilali's son by Joel Chandler Harris—was a "Negro"-despising slaver, had first tried to sell the manuscript. Later in the 1930s, the redoubtable Lydia Parrish— taking cues from the indomitable souls around her on St. Simon's Island, whom she encouraged to sing their peculiar spirituals after a period of quiet—joined with the library's Ella May Thornton to get the "Diary," as it was then called, translated. I will return to this complicated effort later. Perhaps the most important occurrence in the decade was a series of interviews of Georgia ex-slaves that included recollections of Bilali, Salih Bilali, and at least eighteen other African Muslims. I will return later to these as well.

Georgia Sea Island historians liked to write positively about "Mahommetans" or Arab-Africans, whom they preferred to think of as mulattoes rather than full Africans. These slaves were a substantial presence because slave buyers preferred people from Senegambia—the closest point in Africa—where the people supposedly carried themselves with more dignity than elsewhere on the continent. This notion, of course, was a prejudice rather than a fact. Nonetheless, such people were particularly sought after by American slavers during the period between the end of the Revolutionary War and the end of the "legal" international slave trade in January 1808—and beyond, as the Moor on the Mississippi from Chapter 1 and other records show.

A generally misleading prejudice against allowing African American advances of any kind had taken over the country with the slow disintegration of Reconstruction in the 1870s. Some amusing—at first glance wholly fictional and wholly racist, that is, anti-African—stories for children by Harris included a "son of Ben Ali" (the name by which Harris called Bilali). This son, "Aaron," and his father—so sweet to little white children—were presented as nearly white Arabs who found no fault with slavery. Worse yet, they were depicted as despising blacks, whom, Harris's narrator says, they callously captured and sold (*The Story of Aaron {so named}, the Son of Ben Ali*, 1896, and *Aaron in the Wildwoods,* 1897). These attitudes followed those laid out by Harris's very popular and influential character Uncle Remus, who loved slavery times and little white master, who in turn loved his stories of Brer Rabbit. Uncle Remus's "Sayings," found in the back of the books about him, admit no appreciation of schools and political activity for "niggers"—his constant term—especially for those who thought they were as good as white folks. Harris might have done better; elsewhere he wrote positively about "Arabic-Africans" in coastal Georgia, and a Harris reader wrote him in 1890 about an impressive "Arab" slave named Aaron who had a personality that cowed black and white alike. One day this Aaron told his master he wanted no more of slavery and walked away. The impressed master helped him get to Canada, and the two often corresponded with one another. How different from Harris's Aaron and his perversion of history's Bilali.

For a while there was relative silence again. Finally, however, a "Balaly" and other Muslim names sung by Georgia children gave a Muslim spin to Toni Morrison's novel *Song of Solomon* (1977); a Bilali Mahomet, Muslim patriarch, appeared in Julie Dash's movie *Daughters of the Dust* (1992); cultural theorist Ronald A. T. Judy surrounded a partial translation of Bilali's thirteen-page manuscript with a book-length argument that it and Lamine Kebe challenge modernity *{Dis}forming the American Canon* (1993); Africanist Bradford G. Martin offered a partial translation of and commentary on Bilali's manuscript "Sapelo Islands Arabic Document," (1994); historian William S. McFeely, the biographer of Frederick Douglass, finding reason to believe that the latter's original family name—Bailey—might have derived from Bilali, wrote a warm, wandering memoir of recent talks and walks with Bilali's descendants on Sapelo Island, *Sapelo's People*, (1994); historian Michael A. Gomez made Bilali a centerpiece in a wide-ranging article, *Muslims in Early America* (1994); and a gatherer of information related to Islam in America, Muhammad al-Ahari, has been trying to clear up problems in the translation of Bilali's manuscript, forthcoming. Salih Bilali, however, has attracted little attention, although Couper's letter has been reprinted and its African elements annotated by Ivor Wilks "Sahli Bilali of Massina," (1968). There are chapters on each of these men in my previous book.

The name Bilali reflects the West African popularity of the name of the Prophet Muhammad's first *muezzin*, or official summoner to prayer, who was a sweet-voiced Ethiopian liberated from slavery because of his belief in Islam. Both his piety and his emancipation were exemplary, as I noted in Chapter 1. Naturally, this name was popular in West Africa. (Ronald Judy has argued that Bilali should be called Ben Ali, but on flimsy grounds: that Hodgson corrected "Bul-Ali" to "Ben Ali" in 1859; that Harris called him "Ben Ali" in a series of fictional tales, and that the son of Francis Goulding, to whom Bilali gave his manuscript, called him "Ben Ali" in a legal affidavit in 1931. Judy erred in saying that Hodgson, Theodore Dwight Jr. (see Chapter 6) and the younger Goulding met or were otherwise close to Bilali. There is no evidence to support such a conclusion. Couper, who knew both Bilali and Salih Bilali and was careful with his pronunciations, wrote "Sali-bul-Ali" and "Bul-Ali" in 1838;

Georgia Bryan Conrad, who met Bilali and his family in the 1850s—as I noted above—called him "Bi-la-li"; in the 1930s Lydia Parrish heard him referred to as "Belali" by descendants, who also called him "Belali" in Works Project Administration interviews.) Mention of as many as seven Bilalis has been uncovered in records of United States' slaves to date. The Salih in his friend's name probably refers to an ancient prophet named in the Quran, Surahs 7 and 11.

All that is directly known about Bilali's pre-American life may be found in a short comment by his friend Salih Bilali, as recorded by Couper: that he was from Timbo (which I described in Chapter 4), and that Couper thought in the late 1830s that Bilali was "extremely old and feeble," an assertion that two decades of subsequent history seem to contradict. It is unfortunate, however, that no family name or further information about him in Africa was passed on by any contemporaries—including his master, Thomas Spalding, who did write for publication.

Some assumptions may be drawn, however, from Bilali's manuscript and later memories of him. He was probably in the midst of his legal education when he was captured and forced into slavery; his manuscript (two pages of which provide the frontispiece to this chapter) shows that he read and wrote Arabic at a level beyond the basic Quran, but perhaps not far beyond. Once thought to be either a personal or plantation journal, the manuscript has since been characterized as something both less and more.

In 1940, linguist Joseph Greenberg (whose studies of African languages led to his influential reclassification, *The Languages of Africa*, 1963) was prevailed upon by Lydia Parrish (who encouraged a revival of black song on Georgia's "Gullah" islands) and by the leading scholar of African retentions, Melville Herskovitz, to take Bilali's manuscript to Africa for translation. Hausa scholars in Nigeria declared that it was the work of *djinn*, or devils. But with some difficulty, Greenberg concluded that the document consisted of a "title page, portions of the introduction, and parts of . . . chapters dealing with ablutions and the call to prayer" from the *Risala,* composed by abu Muhammad Abdullah bin Zaid al Qairawani before 1011 CE. This is a popular legal commentary of the Malikite school predominant in Muslim West Africa from Morocco to the Gulf of Guinea. Further investigation translates the title as "First Fruits of Happiness," an identification of Islamic law with healthy daily life that is wholly consistent with the ideals of the religion. It is quite possible that Bilali may have been asserting in his American effort—if only to himself—a kind of equality with his American owner, who was a sometime lawyer.

But the manuscript—now in the University of Georgia library—poses many problems. Greenberg could not translate beyond fragments because, he declared, there were too many misspellings. Africanist Bradford Martin, mentioned earlier, has gone a little further in his article on Bilali, his writing, and the paper on which he wrote. He is not convinced that Bilali was recalling Zaid's *Risala* or treatise; he suggests an elementary school text. Because he found a number of rewritings, as well as misspellings, and little order, he is not sure whether this was a schoolboy's effort and therefore composed in Africa or the recollections of an aged man long removed from scholarly peers. Without going into all the details, Martin concludes that the first two pages haphazardly suggest rules about praying. Then there is confusion for about four pages, followed by two pages of easier-to-read rules on ritual washings before prayer. The next five pages are repetitive assertions of faith, hope in being accepted as a servant of God, and comments on times to pray.

This outline accords with the findings of another translator, Muhammad al-Ahari, who finds a clearer introduction to the obligation of prayer and the hopes of the believer. In a yet unpublished effort, he skips from page 2 to page 7, the *Bab*, or the chapter on ablutions and the required prayers. He then brings up a suggestion that is implied in the work of Kebe and London: that some of Bilali's misspellings may be due to his writing Pular or Fulfulde—the language of the Fulbe—with Arabic characters.

Along with some mechanical notes, Ronald Judy finds at least two hands at work: one for pages 1 through 4, another for the remaining pages, and perhaps another (an editor) in the marginalia. He also finds that at least one page is missing between the present pages 6 and 7. His translation does not go beyond the pages covered by al-Ahari, but it does suggest in a phrase that the writer has been ordered or has taken as an order the obligation to write what follows: "Write me books that are a brief exposition. . . ." In a roundabout way, Judy also explores the possibility of Pular-Arabic writing in Bilali's manuscript. He concludes that the work is a mix of classical Arabic like that found in writings by Job, Abd ar-Rahman, and Umar: Pular Arabic reflecting Pular pronunciations; and Pular written with the phonetic Arabic characters. Unfortunately, Judy does not prove this suggestion in his translation.

A lengthy discourse on several levels of Arabic heterography leads, however, to an assertion that the manuscript's African-Arabic script is—on a level where Judy may be taken seriously—the opposite of a self-conscious European autobiography or slave narrative: it is a sign of authority in the Muslim way because it reflects spiritual truths passed on to those who can repeat them. When Judy declares that the work also establishes the writer as being above other slaves ("as not-being-nigger"), he is surely correct, though the terminology is ugly. When Judy tacks on two more chapters to show that Kant and Western philosophy are made dumb by Bilali's text, he is straining far beyond the simple point made in Chapter 1 of this book: that there are texts and people in America that have deserved and will repay attention surpassing the common presumptions about Africans and African Americans.

Martin traced the paper itself to Venetian producers who exported to North Africa in the late eighteenth century. This finding that the paper must have been brought from Africa lends credence to the traditional stories that describe Bilali as being buried with his Quran and prayer rug, which must also have come from Africa. These facts suggest that Bilali was an unusually strong individual.

For Bilali, between Africa and Georgia fell the shadows of the Middle Passage and a stay of indefinite length in the Bahamas. Bilali either brought with him or there married one or more wives (four are legitimate in Islam). His purchaser Thomas Spalding seems to have recognized the leader and perhaps the experienced rice grower in Bilali and brought him to the mainland with a then-unknown number of sons and seven daughters. There were already French-speaking slaves on the islands. Muslims did not usually learn European languages until doing so appeared advantageous, but it is reported that all but Bilali's daughter could speak English, French, Fulfulde, and perhaps Arabic.

Georgia Bryan Conrad's description of Bilali and his Muslim dress was followed by the assertion that "They conversed with us in English, but in talking among themselves they used a foreign tongue that no one else understood."

She added that the whole family "worshipped Mahomet" and that they "held themselves aloof from the others as if they were conscious of their own superiority." This last remark demonstrates that most whites saw this attitude of pride as a sense of being better than other blacks. But "the others" undoubtedly included non-Muslim whites as well.

The one who knew Bilali best, perhaps, after Salih Bilali was Bilali's owner. Slave and master seem to have been fortunate in finding each other. In 1794, Thomas Spalding (1774–1851) inherited $20,000 from his father, James Spalding, a pioneer American cotton grower. A year later, at the age of twenty-one, he was admitted to the bar and married a local beauty. Because his father was a Loyalist, he spent the Revolutionary War years in Scotland and did not return to Georgia until 1802 after having negotiated a loan of $50,000. With this money Spalding bought four thousand acres on the south end of Sapelo Island and invested in slaves—including, presumably, Bilali and his

Fig. 14.   Thomas Spalding, from E. Merton Coulter, *Thomas Spalding of Sapelo,*
frontispiece.

family, as he bought some slaves in Charleston and some in the West Indies. It is reported that he neither sold nor purchased any slaves after 1819. Eventually, his slaves numbered four hundred to one thousand, depending on the source of information.

It was Spalding's plan to treat his slaves like serfs. Each had his own land to work; labor for the master was limited to six hours a day; and slaves worked by the task system—a fairly common practice on the islands off Georgia, where slaves significantly outnumbered freemen. Slave villages (something Bilali's people were used to in Africa) were built in several places, with huts plastered inside and out; each village was placed under a head man; and each ten new people were placed under seasoned, older slaves. Spalding used no white head men and apparently did well. As well as cotton, sugar, and rice crops, he and his people provided timber for ships for the youthful U.S. Navy. By 1832 there were only two owners of Sapelo Island; shortly after 1843, there was only Spalding.

This very profitable plantation and its regimen attracted some attention. It was visited and described by John D. Legare, editor of the *Southern Agriculturist*, in 1832. Seven years later, Spalding's home was again visited, and this time it was negatively assessed. The English actress Fanny Kemble Butler thought Mrs. Spalding, her house, and her life oppressively dull. Legare, Kemble, and others would describe at greater length and with greater appreciation the similar plantation of John and James Hamilton Couper, owner of Bilali's friend Salih Bilali. Spalding's intellectual and political life also attracted some attention. He often wrote for the journals of the day, usually on plantation matters; he collected a large library; he helped frame the state constitution and served in the state Senate and House of Representatives. One of his last acts was an attempt to keep Georgia's Union sentiment strong in December 1850—a month before he died.

But all was not well in the Spalding empire. His wife gave birth to sixteen children, but only seven, all girls, survived infancy. Sarah Spalding apparently tried to be good to her "people"—as the slaves were called—but the wearisome, tedious life referred to by Fanny Kemble Butler led to her early death in 1839. The lack of more numerous and vigorous progeny was one matter that greatly disheartened the dynasty-minded Spalding. But he seems also to have suffered from some mysterious malady about which he wrote in 1844, calling it "a painful disease, of ten years standing."

His two most definitive biographers disagree somewhat on his personality. Caroline Lovell, drawing heavily on an earlier work by one of Spalding's descendants, Charles Spalding Wylly, declared that he was a stern man who disapproved of music, dancing, and card playing—a pen portrait that matches the painting reproduced here of a dour gentleman. He was "absolute in his opinions, domineering even to his children until he went to the point of violating all custom and became in the end a law unto himself." This conclusion is not supported by any examples of tyrannical behavior, but it seems to indicate a family feeling. On the other hand, a few pages later, Lovell argues that Spalding was generally a decent man.

Lovell also claimed that Spalding had no sense of humor. At least once, however, he seems to have wittily united a practical need with thoughts about his slave foreman. Sugar-processing implements had to be carefully tended, he said, "for no Mahometan with his seven daily ablutions, is a greater enemy to dirt than sugar is." The publisher of this sally, Spalding's latest biographer, E. Merton Coulter, proffered a predominantly congenial portrait, summing up his character thus: "stern, quick-tempered, and ardent, yet tender, affectionate and generous and a most considerate master"—who did, perhaps, prefer to live in the past. His slaves' opinion was not recorded.

He had no son to take over, and his property shrank. It was not until 1870, five years after the Civil War ended, that the plantation that had been abandoned to Sapelo Island's African Americans—or "runaway Negroes"—was taken over by "young Tom" (a grandson), and the former slaves were "dislodged with some difficulty." Some of this history is told in McFeely's book *Sapelo's People.* Even there the story is not complete, but the book does tell how Tom's lack of success led to the island's being left to Bilali's descendants.

The Savannah Unit of the Georgia Writers Project of the Works Projects Administration (WPA) interviewed many ex-slaves and published their responses in 1940 in a book called *Drums and Shadows,* referred to in Chapter 1. The title refers to the many stories that recall the persistence of drummers and the fear of shadows, or "hants" (the shades of ancestors), and other native African beliefs. The book might have been called *Dances, Drums, Shadows, and Flying Africans.* Stories like these, including flying Africans and several Muslim names (Solomon, Balaly, Medina, Omar, Ryna, Muhammet), play a prominent part in Toni Morrison's novel *Song of Solomon,* as noted elsewhere.

This quartet of themes suggests areas where the interests of masters and slaves might conflict. Bilali's master did not interfere, apparently, with practices his Africans considered their right. This policy was not always the case in Georgia, as may be seen in the example of Salih Bilali's St. Simon's Island.

Fig. 15. Bilali Descendant Shad Hall of Sapelo, late 1930s, from *Drums and Shadows,* 1940.

The description in *Drums and Shadows* of the Sapelo Island of the 1930s includes the recollections of Katie Brown (Fig. 16), granddaughter of Margaret, daughter of Bilali, and of Shadrach (Shad) Hall (Fig. 15), grandson of Hester, Margaret's sister. Bilali sired five other daughters: Charlotte (Cotty), Fatima, Yoruba (or Nyrubuh), Medina, and Binty. Fatima and Medina are distinctively

Fig. 16. Bilali Descendant Katie Brown of Sapelo, late 1930s, from *Drums and Shadows*, 1940.

Muslim names. Neither of these two descendants gave the name of his or her father. Katie Brown (born about 1851) said all of Bilali's daughters were born before he arrived in America. He and one of his wives, Phoebe, from the Bahamas, prayed with beads, about which they were very particular, at very specific times: "Bilali he pull back and he say, 'Belambi, Hakebera Mahamadia'" (a compression of "God is one, great" and "Mohammed is his prophet"). Bilali had his own prayer rug too. Phoebe made the ceremonial *saraka* (honey and rice) cake for the end of fasting at Ramadan and for harvest time. She clearly knew French and was probably from Senegal. Her supposedly African words, "deloe" and "diffy," are probably *de l'eau* (water) and *de feu* (fire).

Shad Hall, younger than Katie Brown, talked about a man who must have been Bilali, although Hall seems to say that he himself worked for the Marquis de Montalet as a boy before working for young Tom and then Mike Spalding as Hall did. Perhaps both men worked for the Marquis. Hall had been told that Bilali was "coal-black," very tall, and had small "feechuhs." He named Bilali's daughters too (one of whom, Fatima, was named for her mother, according to another source) and described Bilali's and Hester's praying, the latter's recollections of houses and food in Africa (or the Bahamas?), and the *saraka* she used to make. Hall also spoke of conjuring, shouts, harvest festivals, funerals, shadows, working hoes, flying Africans, An Nancy (Anansi, the spider hero), and an uncle named Bilali Smith (a second-generation Muslim, perhaps).

Reuben Grovernor, another descendant of Bilali, was famous for his un-Islamic Buzzard Lope dance, which may have originated in Africa. Some others recalled African Muslim ancestors whose geographical provenance is less certain. Julia Grovernor recalled Calina and Hannah, her grandparents. Hannah was caught digging peanuts in Africa, tied up in a sack, and put on a ship to America. Phoebe Gilbert told of Calina's being taken from a beach to which he had been enticed by red cloth. Both were called Ibos, but they were probably not the Ibo people of the land now called Nigeria but "Hebos," or partly Islamicized people living near the Atlantic Coast south of the Gambia River. They shared this "nationality" with a people who were remembered for having flown back to Africa. Gilbert said Calina and Hannah and Bilali Smith were her grandparents, and Nero Jones recalled that the first pair prayed at particular times and used Muslim prayer beads: "Duh ole man he say 'Ameela' an An [Aunt] Hannah she say 'Hakebera.'" These people had probably become full Muslims under Bilali's tutelage. Muslims apparently married one another on Sapelo Island at least into a second generation.

Finally, another probable Spalding slave from Africa was remembered by Ed Thorpe of Harris Neck, on mainland Georgia. Patience Spalding, his grandmother, he recalled, was also attracted into slavery by a red cloth. He remembered her praying: "She kneel down on duh flo. She bow uh head down tree time and she say 'Ameen, Ameen, Ameen'"—as Muslims were taught to do. These remembrances contradict the tradition that Bilali's children were Christians.

They also suggest how far his island people became Muslims. Without a second-generation *imam*, their spiritual lives probably combined several traditions, but this theory and these people need to be seriously studied by Muslim as well as non-Muslim investigators.

More information about Bilali and his family and their Muslim ways may yet be found. Those Afro-Americans who did recall Bilali and his peculiar habits remembered them as narrated by women. Here women seem to be the carriers of their people's traditions, and perhaps this practice was more often the case among Muslims than has hitherto been recognized. This tradition might also, of course, be because the interviewers and interviewees were largely female. The lack of such interviews earlier in time has created a gap in information on female African Muslims.

One must wonder what happened to Bilali's twelve sons. Where did they fly to? and why? It may also be noticed that although these former-slave sources thought of Bilali as a cultural ancestor, none mentioned his having been a writer. Perhaps they were less impressed with this skill than Euro-Americans, or, possibly, Bilali himself.

Meanwhile, back on St. Simon's Island in the late 1830s, one of the more famous Sea Island proprietors, James Hamilton Couper, was urged by his friend, a fellow plantation owner and earlier sojourner in North Africa, William Brown Hodgson, to seriously consider his head driver as an ethnological specimen. Perhaps no other person could have gotten Couper to do so. Their views on slavery and on the Fulbe—Salih Bilali's and Bilali's people—of whom Hodgson often wrote admiringly but not always correctly (for example, he assumed their virtues were attributable to white blood), were similar. It may also have been Hodgson who suggested that Couper try to find a drawing of someone who looked like Salih Bilali in an early ethnological study by the avowed abolitionist James C. Prichard. Couper did, and it is reproduced here (see Fig. 17). The other portrait is a photo of Salih Bilali's grandson, Ben Sullivan, which nearly perfectly reflects Couper's description of his head driver.

It seems clear that Salih Bilali was a shrewd and self-respecting man. From 1816 to 1846, he directed from three hundred to five hundred workers on plantations where cotton, rice, sweet potatoes, cowpeas, corn, and sugarcane (crops that were the same as or similar to those grown in his West Africa) and their rotation (as well as olive trees and date palms) were experimented with under the supervision of this watchful African-born driver or manager. Couper wrote

Fig. 17. Salih Bilali Look-alike—According to James H. Couper, 1842, "Native of Hausa" from James C. Prichard, *Illustrations to the Researches into the Physical History of Mankind,* 1844.

that his head man did very well (like Spalding and Bilali) when the master left for months at a time.

One wonders what kind of driver he was: the unfeeling tyrant who enjoyed lording it over slaves—as some white overseers did—a merciless African over other Africans, a type referred to often by Southerners and horrendously imagined by the editors of anti–Abd ar-Rahman newspapers, as we saw in Chapter 4, or the Fula accustomed to ordering around non-Fulbe *kufrs,* or unbelievers. If so, he might well have agreed with Bilali's harsh remark about the unrelia-

Fig. 18.   Descendant Ben Sullivan, St. Simon's Island, 1938, from Margaret Davis Cate, *Early Days in Coastal Georgia*, 1955, p. 154.

bility of the non-Fulbe slaves. He was undoubtedly a complex figure, working for master, slaves, and self, as historians Eugene Genovese and Leslie Howard Owens have attempted to describe in their slave studies. It is clear that his was a position of authority and responsibility. He probably earned respect through careful attention to details and possibly aroused fear of various sorts, but there allegedly was little whipping on this plantation.

Salih Bilali, like Bilali and Abd ar-Rahman, was surely, as one writer aptly if condescendingly opined about black drivers in general, "a patriarch who held rule over his tribe"—a tribe that was probably more ethnically diverse on the American side of the Atlantic than on the other. The Fulbe had slave villages in Africa for field laborers, personal servants, and military uses, but Salih Bilali would not have had a difficult time explaining the difference between the apparently unrequited labor of Massina's nonfree castes and Georgia's chattel slaves. The former worked in their own fields for part of the week; they had homes, clothes, and village organizations of their own that were similar to those of their masters; they had recognized rights to property, wives and children, and religious and secular education not allowed in Georgia. Some might also gain their freedom and continue to live in the neighborhood thereafter.

It is possible that both Salih Bilali and Bilali were responsible for a flowering of the Fula language in this part of Georgia, perhaps as a result of their powerful positions. It was said that several other slaves who knew the language lived close by. Does this fact not suggest a greater Fula influence in the formation of the local Gullah culture than has hitherto been recognized? At least eighteen African Muslims and perhaps Fulbe related to the Couper or Spalding estates were located for WPA interviewers in the 1930s.

Salih Bilali's masters, first John Couper (1759–1850) and then his son James Hamilton Couper (1794–1866), were as well known as Bilali's Thomas Spalding, in their case for their hospitality and mostly successful plantations: Cannon's Point on St. Simon's Island and Hopeton on the Altamaha River, Georgia. Thus, they attracted some of the same domestic and foreign sightseers. Aaron Burr visited the elder Couper in 1804. A Royal Navy captain and explorer, Basil Hall, and his not easily impressed wife, Margaret Hunter Hall—both formidable travelers and writers—visited John and James Couper in 1828. The captain wrote about the reasonable task system used for growing the superior Sea Island cotton and added notes on the necessary despotism required on slave plantations, which he likened to that found in "ships of war, many regiments, and, I fear, I may add, many domestic establishments, to say nothing of schools." His wife thought that the son's house was "the very smallest that we have been in, a mere pigeon-hole," but she believed that it had more order and more books than most larger "enterprises" she had visited. When John D. Legare, the founder and editor of the *Southern Agriculturist*—interested in production and profits—visited the younger Couper, whose careful management inspired him to write nine articles on nearly every aspect of coastal Georgia plantation life, in 1833, he admired Hopeton and saw it as a "large white mansion." Apparently it had been enlarged. He considered the role of black overseers several times but did not refer to Salih Bilali directly.

The British actress and American critic Fanny Kemble Butler was a neighbor for a short while in 1838–1839. She immediately liked the elder Couper and his treatment of slaves but became disheartened on a second visit when he expanded on Africans' lack of capacity to be other than slaves. She was even more upset by the son's absolute control, including such practices as withholding meat from slaves to keep them from committing "crimes of a savage nature." I will discuss other forms of control later. Kemble also alluded to but did not elaborate upon a matter not discussed by other writers on the Coupers: "It must not be forgotten that on the estate of this wise and kind master a formidable conspiracy was organized among his slaves." One wonders what role Salih Bilali played in that plot.

British geologist Charles Lyell enjoyed the plantation's bounty and its master's hospitality and culture in 1842. He was also interested in slave-master relations, but not critically. He concluded that those relations on the Couper plantations were amiable. He enjoyed the names of some slaves, including "Bullaly," probably one of Salih Bilali's sons. He did meet Salih Bilali, who was introduced as head driver "Tom" in his plantation role. He called "Tom" a prince, retold some of his African history, and stated that he "remained a strict Mahometan." He was also informed—maybe by Salih Bilali—about the head man's partially successful attempts to keep slaves from running to the British in 1815 by telling them that slavery in the Bahamas was worse than in America. Nonetheless, half of the slaves chose to leave the Couper paradise—a decision that later writers attributed to British force. Lyell also said that Salih Bilali's "jet-black children and grandchildren" had all become Christians. He was probably no more correct in this matter than he was in others concerning this African. He went on to easy denigrations of "Africanians," while contradictorily admiring the skills of local black singers and mechanics and presuming that they were being encouraged to become more literate and more Christian. That hope was groundless.

Swedish novelist Fredrika Bremer visited in 1851, liked the younger Couper, and decided that "the institution of slavery [was] a benefit" to Africans. The Victorian courtier Amelia M. Murray was also delighted with what she saw there in 1855, and she essentially repeated Bremer's conclusion.

It is unfortunate, and curious, that only one of these visitors, Lyell, seems to have been introduced to Salih Bilali or to any other individual slaves. However, this purportedly enlightened slave master may not have cared to publicize or to let anyone else publicize his remarkable African.

The most detailed source of information on Salih Bilali was written by his master to William Brown Hodgson, who had asked for some particulars about

Fig. 19.   John Couper. Photo of oil portrait, courtesy of Mrs. Mary Thiesen, a direct descendant.

Couper's black overseer, or head driver, who was known as a responsible plantation manager and an apparently devout Muslim. The letter emphasizes its subject's Old World history and, naturally, qualities in the man that were useful to Couper's needs and temperament. As such, it is important for its nearly unique descriptions of Niger River social and economic life two hundred miles southwest of Timbuktu in the 1770s and 1780s—and its depiction of Salih Bilali.

Fig. 20.   James Hamilton Couper. Photo of oil portrait, courtesy of Mrs. Mary Thiesen, a direct descendant.

For his Islamic training to have been as impressive as Couper says before he was taken away at the age of fourteen, Salih Bilali must have received very good early schooling in Massina and perhaps some additional training under Muslim teachers, possibly even Bilali, in the Bahamas. There are undoubtedly stories yet to be told about Georgia-Bahamas slaveholder and slave connections.

Couper added only a little more of this man's history. He was clearly an impressive figure, according to Couper, who did not regularly allow things African much credit. Let me borrow from Couper: Of "about a dozen who spoke the Foulah [Pular or Fulfulde] language" on Hopeton plantation, only "Tom" was a native speaker. Others had learned it as slaves of the Fulbe, opined Couper, even though he later wrote, erroneously, that the Fulbe had had no slaves in Africa. "Tom [born around 1765], whose African name was Sali-bul-Ali, was purchased about the year 1800, by my father, from the Bahama islands, to which he had been brought [around 1780] from Anamaboo [present-day Ghana]." (At a later point, Couper described him as being "brownish black" with "woolly" hair.) Couper continued, "His industry, intelligence, and honesty, soon brought him into notice, and he was successively advanced, until he was made head driver of this plantation, in 1816. He has continued in that station ever since, having under him a gang of about four hundred and fifty negroes, which number, he has shown himself fully competent to manage with advantage. I have several times left him for months, in charge of the plantation, without an overseer; and on each occasion, he has conducted the place to my entire satisfaction."

Couper praised his head man's "quickness of apprehension, strong powers of combination and calculation, a sound judgment, a singularly tenacious memory, and what is more rare in a slave, the faculty of forethought. He possesses great veracity and honesty. He is a strict Mahometan; abstains from spiritous liquors, and keeps the various fasts, particularly that of the Rhamadam." Later one of Couper's sons said Salih Bilali "was the most religious man that he had ever known," declaring further that the exiled Salih Bilali on his deathbed proudly proclaimed: "Allah is God and Mohammed his prophet."

Couper had told enough about his man's American life, apparently, and turned to the seventy-three-year-old's reminiscences of Africa. Salih Bilali told Couper about the large town of Kianah that was his birthplace, distant from "Tumbootu" (Timbuktu), near the Niger River—called the Mayo by the Fula—to the northeast and close to "Jennay" (Jenne) to the southwest. Both were famous Muslim intellectual centers. Further to the southwest was "Sego" (Segu), described in 1795 as a grand city by the explorer Mungo Park, through which Salih Bilali would be marched to the coast after his kidnapping. Houses were made of dried mud or brick or heavy grass, and those of religious leaders were not larger than ordinary homes. Salih Bilali was from a well-to-do family and had been taught to read Arabic, as he said all Fulbe in Kianah were, but not to write it. He was undoubtedly taken away before he reached that level.

Arab traders who traveled in forty-boat convoys along the river had impressed the youth. They traded salt, "blankets, guns, pistols, cotton cloth, beads, shell money [cowries] and sometimes horses." The Fulbe raised "horses, cows, sheep for wool, goats, and some asses. They grew rice, several grains, beans, gourds, okra, tomatoes, cucumbers, cotton, cocoanuts, pineapples, figs and indigo for blue dye." Grains, cotton, rice, and indigo were all export crops in the United States, and Africans with experience growing such crops were sought after. Most Europeans had not had experience with these crops. This point has been explored only by the most recent generation of scholars.

Salih Bilali may have been trying to make a point when he declared that in Africa women did not work in the fields as female slaves were forced to do in the United States. He may have been trying to say something else when he led Couper to write that there were no slaves in Massina—perhaps he meant that there were no Muslim slaves. There certainly were non-Muslim slaves. Ideally, of course, if a slave converted to Islam he could be freed, like the Prophet Muhammad's Bilali. This principle may or may not have been put into practice at the whim of Muslim leaders, according to Christian historians. However, it may be pointed out that even on the best of Christian plantations—including Couper's, according to Fanny Kemble Butler—little attention was paid to the religion of the slaves, and there was no prospect of conversion leading to their emancipation.

Couper said that Salih Bilali was captured by Bambaras while riding a horse back from Jenne and was then marched to the coast some 500 miles away. After he left Bambara country, which had been influenced by Islam, Salih Bilali claimed that there were no more religious people and some cannibals near the coast. It has been common, of course, to call strangers cannibals, as Odysseus did when he looked across the water to the underdeveloped land of the Cyclops.

Finally, before appending a haphazard list of thirty-five Fulfulde words and translations, Couper described Salih Bilali as an adult: "In his personal appearance, Tom is tall, thin, but well made. His features are small, forehead well developed, mouth well formed, with lips less protruding than is usual with the negro race, the nose flat, but not thick. His eyes are peculiar, being like those of a Chinese, without their obliquity. The portrait of a native of 'Hausa,' in Prichard's *Natural History of Man*, gives the general character of his head and face, and approaches more nearly to it, than that of any other given of the African tribes." This portrait is reproduced here (see Figure 17).

Couper seemed to have completed his duty to his friend and to his slave foreman with the completion of this letter. As far as I have been able to discover, he wrote no more about Salih Bilali.

Couper had nothing to say about the part Salih Bilali may have played in a slave conspiracy that Fanny Kemble Butler's husband mentioned as taking place on his plantation, nor about what part his head man may have played in an unsuccessful experiment that gave some Couper slaves land of their own to cultivate and profit from. He could not have said anything about how Salih Bilali died and whether it happened, as one of the latter's descendants recalled, on his way to or from engineering a slave purchase on a nearby island.

James H. Couper was a methodical man, and, as he wrote in his letter, he found Salih Bilali to be one also. Couper held to a rigid daily regime. By a systematic use of his time, he was able to cultivate his scientific tastes, and correspondence with him was solicited by many learned societies.

Hodgson wrote that Salih Bilali died late in the 1850s, but he may have confused the two Bilalis. At about the same time, Couper retired from his management of Hopeton and in 1857 moved to Altama, a smaller tabby home he had designed and landscaped. The retirement party was announced, we are told, by "Bulala"—surely Salih Bilali's son, as may be confirmed from the memories of his descendants.

All of Couper's six sons volunteered for the war. Two died of sickness during the war, one became a hermit after it, and another's long imprisonment proved very damaging. Couper himself contracted large debts during the war. By the end he had lost his plantation and had nothing left to live for. He died in 1866, and neither Hopeton nor Altama was successfully cultivated thereafter.

Early in the war, after slaveholders had fled from many of the Georgia Sea Islands, a military company of African Americans (all that remained after Lincoln rejected the idea of the colored Hunter Regiment, the unauthorized First South Carolina Volunteer Regiment) was told to garrison St. Simon's Island and that it would have to first capture or destroy a group of rebel guerrillas. In August 1862, they found that a local but black John Brown—his real name—and his men had already been fighting against the rebels for ten days. The leader of the rebel group was later to write, "If you wish to know hell before your time, go to St. Simon's Island and be hunted ten days by niggers." Were some of these "hunters" offspring of Salih Bilali? If so, they may be credited with being involved in what was the first armed encounter "between the rebels and their former slaves." This incident was described by Thomas Wentworth Higginson in his famous book of personal observations, *Army Life in a Black Regiment*. At least one other Southerner, William McFeely, also recognized that many Sea Islanders joined the U.S. Army during the war.

After the war, several people remembered something about Salih Bilali and the "good old days." The recollections of whites tended to smooth over any rough spots. Slavery was recalled as being an imperfect but necessary system for the not-too-healthy land and the supposedly not-too-civilized African laborers who provided the economic basis for the life of the sometime wealthy and sometime cultured master class. The memories of blacks—when finally elicited from people who were not sure of the uses whites might make of them—are more critical. The former slaves remembered James Couper's attempts to place limits on their predecessors' lives, but they also remembered the passing on of African names, words, and traditions. Salih Bilali's family did not die out with the end of slavery. Unfortunately, however, no one seems to have been asked to recall this ancestor in detail.

The Georgia Writers Project found some of Salih Bilali's descendants on St. Simon's Island in the 1930s. Many told the same stories that the Sapelo Island ex-slaves had told, but it is clear that Couper tried to control more of his slaves' cultural lives than did Spalding. It is also clear that Couper did not succeed. More detailed information has been discovered about Salih Bilali than about Bilali. His grandson, Ben Sullivan, was a spry eighty-eight years old when the photograph accompanying this chapter was taken (Fig. 18). Ben recalled his father, who had apparently been given the Arabic name, Bilali, by his father, Salih Bilali, and who had been allowed to keep it by master Couper. Bilali was, Sullivan recalled, Couper's butler at Altama plantation, to which Couper retired in 1857. He also remembered his father making *saraka,* or rice cakes (whereas, it will be recalled, the women did so on Sapelo Island), which were related to Muslim ceremonies in Africa and then in America. After emancipation for an as yet undiscovered reason, Bilali took the name Sullivan rather than Couper, the surname of his master.

About his grandfather Sullivan could only remember—or was only pushed to remember—that his "fathuh's fathuh wuz a unmarried man," and more intriguing yet, that he once went to Dungeness on Cumberland Island (south of St. Simon's) to trade in slaves and was never seen again. Thereby must hang a tale, but I have not found it. Did Salih Bilali die by the hand of some enemy? Sullivan seems to have said no more about him.

Ben Sullivan did have several things to say, however, about other Muslims and about the Coupers. Okra, Gibson, and Israel belonged to James Couper, "talked funny," and talked about having built their own camp in Africa. At least one of them, Okra, tried to do the same in America. He wanted "a place lak he hab in Africa," so he built a hut of mud and palm fronds. Couper made him pull it down, saying "he ain wahn no African hut on he place." Nor did Couper want drums. Another slave, Dembo, used to beat a drum for funerals until he was told to stop. Sullivan remembered that yet another slave, Jesse, and

Okra were both good drum makers. They must have played in the master's absence. Several of Couper's slaves did not put Africa and Islam completely behind them. Israel, Sullivan said, prayed, from a book he kept hidden, on a mat at sunrise and sunset. He had sharp features, a long, pointed beard, was "bery tall," and tied his head up in a white cloth. Both Daphne, also sharp featured, but light in color, and Alexander Boyd, Sullivan's mother's father (dark and sharp featured), used to "tie up" their heads and pray three times a day. With so many African-oriented people around, it seems likely that wishes for things African (Islamic?) were a possible cause of the conspiracy on the Couper plantation to which Fanny Kemble Butler's husband referred.

Sullivan also remembered Hettie, mother of his mother, Bella; both women, he thought, were African. Whether from Africa or the Bahamas, he recalled that Hettie had said she was glad to leave, although she was bothered by the new language and worried about relatives left behind. This is the only case I know of where the obvious forced migrant's anxiety seems to have been mentioned, though this time experienced by an African. He also remembered Bilali's mother's name: Luna. It is possible that this was the same woman whom another Couper slave descendant, Charles Hunter (very black of skin and rather small featured), recalled as Louise, his grandmother, who was from the Bahamas. Or was this a second wife to Salih Bilali? Hunter also remembered Alexander, a conjurer and doctor who could fly, perhaps the Alexander Boyd mentioned elsewhere.

Ryna Johnson (probably the "Rina" who worked for the Coupers and was found at Cannon's Point by James Couper's son sixteen years after he left the plantation in 1857), about eighty-five when interviewed, recalled good times at the Coupers'. She also recalled singing and drums and three Africans: Alexander, "Jummy," and William, who had all been entrapped by their passion for red cloth and who used the same African words, "Sojo," "deloe," and "diffy," as Margaret, daughter of Spalding's Bilali. Ryna's husband, not coincidentally, was from Sapelo Island. Rosa Grant—another Salih Bilali descendant—described a Ryna who seems to have been an older person. This Ryna prayed at sunup, touching her head to the floor and saying a prayer that included such expressions as "ashamnegad" and "Ameen, Ameen, Ameen" (Muslim "amen"). Grant also recalled that Ryna prayed on Fridays and celebrated a feast day, noting, probably, the end of Ramadan. She thought that Ryna had been captured and sold with her mother.

Finally, near Couper's Altama, Rachel and Alec Anderson recalled harvest festivals, the Buzzard Lope dance, shouts, and a dance called "come down tuh duh Myuh"—another name for the Niger. It appears that such dances were

frowned upon by Fula elders. Rachel Anderson recalled a more sober grandmother, Peggy, who prayed every day at sunrise, noon, and sunset, facing the
sun, and who insisted on certain dietary prohibitions.

The Georgia Sea Island informants from St. Simon's and Sapelo Island
mentioned in this chapter seem to have been proud of their predecessors. Like
Bilali, Salih Bilali clearly passed on many of his racial characteristics and,
apparently despite his master's disapproval, African traditions. He and Bilali
may have been more influential in the creation of Gullah culture than has hitherto been recognized. Perhaps more might have been discovered about his
"rough and ready" ways had his descendants felt free to tell all of what they
remembered. Even so, it appears that at least twenty midcentury African
Muslims were readily recalled as late in time as the World War II era on these
two islands alone.

There was one character described in the WPA studies who might link
past and present Muslims. One preacher—and we need to find out what he
was preaching—mightily impressed some interviewers. They wrote, "The
preacher came from behind the platform and stood silently behind the pulpit
desk, looking dramatically over his congregation. He was tall and spare, with
brown skin, narrow face, and a thin pointed beard, a Mohammedan looking
Negro. He wore a black skull cap, which we learned later was not ritualistic but
was worn to protect his head from the draught. This was preacher Little who,
we were afterwards told, was an itinerant preacher, not a native to the island but
a type native to the district." To the interviewers, the compelling element was
less what he said than the sound of Preacher Little's voice. More information
about him needs to be found.

SELECTED READINGS

Hodgson read the letter from Couper before the American Ethnological Society
sometime in 1843 and published it in his *Notes on Northern Africa, the Sahara,
and the Soudan* (New York, 1844), 68–75. Hodgson (1801–1871), a Georgia
plantation owner mentioned often in this book, held two honorary degrees
from Princeton and served in the U.S. consulates of Algiers (1826–1829),
Constantinople (1832–1834), and Tunis (1841–1842). He was a founder of
the American Oriental Society and a member of the American Philosophical and
Ethnological Societies. See Leonard L. MacKall, "William Brown Hodgson"
(an attempt at a life and biography), *Georgia Historical Quarterly* 19, no. 15
(December 1931), 324–345.

Hodgson's racial views may be found in his *Notes* and in a pamphlet, "The

Foulahs of Central Africa and the African Slave Trade" (New York [apparently published by the author], 1843): "The Foulahs are not Negroes . . . [They are] a distinct race, in moral as in physical traits." They were, he said, superior and white (pp. 4–5). He erred here, as the blacker Fulbe were the more sedentary and literate, as I noted earlier. To Hodgson "the Negro" was, of course, barbarous (p. 14). But Hodgson appears to have come around later. In 1858, in a rare pamphlet, he wrote about the "Songhay, Foolah, and other powerful negro races of the Niger" met by Heinrich Barth (see Chapter 9).

Hodgson, also the translator of one of Abd ar-Rahahman's manuscripts (see above p. 75, n. 137), was described by John Davidson, Abu Bakr's companion heading for Timbuktu, as the two men met in Gibraltar in 1835: "the most gentleman-like American I have ever seen. . . . He improves much upon acquaintance." *Notes Taken During Travels in Africa* (London: privately printed, 1839), 4–5.

Hodgson in America was also described by a *London Times* correspondent during the Civil War (p. 64). At breakfast in Hodgson's home, he saw "in attendance some good-looking Negro boys and men dressed in liveries, which smacked of our host's Orientalism." William H. Russell, *My Diary, North and South* (New York: Harper, 1863).

Margaret Davis Cate, *Early Days of Coastal Georgia* (St. Simon's Island, Ga.: Fort Frederica Association, 1955).

Georgia Bryan Conrad, *Reminiscences of a Southern Woman* (Hampton, Virginia: Hampton Institute, n.d. [1901?]).

E. Merton Coulter, *Thomas Spalding of Sapelo* (Baton Rouge: Louisiana State University, 1940).

Philip D. Curtin, *Economic Change in Pre-Colonial Africa* (Madison: University of Wisconsin Press, 1975.

For the role of overseers and black drivers, see Eugene Genovese, *Roll, Jordan, Roll: The World the Slaves Made* (New York: Pantheon, 1974) and Leslie H. Owens, *This Species of Property: Slave Life and Culture in the Old South* (New York: Oxford University Press, 1976).

George Gerster, "River of Sorrow, River of Hope," *National Geographic Magazine* 148, no. 2 (August 1975), 162–164, provides pictures of the Niger that would have been recognizable to Salih Bilali.

Michael A. Gomez, "Muslims in Early America," *Journal of Southern History* 60 (November 1994), 671–709.

For Africans from the same area of Africa, see also Gwendolyn Midlo Hall, *Africans in Colonial Louisiana: The Development of Afro-Creole Culture in the 18th Century* (Baton Rouge: Louisiana State University Press, 1992).

Thomas W. Higginson, *Army Life in a Black Regiment* (1867) (reprinted New York: Collier, 1962).

Ronald A. T. Judy, *(Dis)Forming the American Canon: African-Arabic Slave Narratives and the Vernacular* (Minneapolis: University of Minnesota Press, 1993).

Caroline Couper Lovell (a direct descendant of the Coupers), *The Golden Isles of Georgia* (Boston: Little, Brown, 1933). This book is largely a rewriting of Charles Spalding Wylly's interesting and romantic *Seed That Was Sown in the Colony of Georgia, the Harvest and Aftermath, 1740–1870* (New York: Neale, 1910). The "seed" was slavery.

Charles Lyell, *A Second Visit to the United States of North America* (New York: Harper, 1849).

B[radford] G. Martin, "Sapelo Island's Arabic Document . . . in Context," *Georgia Historical Quarterly* (Fall 1994), 589–601.

William S. McFeely, *Sapelo's People: A Long Walk into Freedom* (New York: Norton, 1994).

Amelia M. Murray, *Letters from the United States, Cuba, and Canada* (New York: Putnam, 1856).

Lydia Parrish, *Slave Songs of the Georgia Sea Islands* (New York: Creative Age, 1942).

James C. Prichard, *Researches into the Physical History of Mankind*, 4th ed., vol. 2 (London: Houlston and Stoneham, 1851).

Savannah Unit of the Georgia Writers Project of the Works Projects Administration, *Drums and Shadows: Survival Studies Among the Georgia Coastal Negroes* (1940) (reprinted Athens: University of Georgia Press, 1986).

John A. Scott, ed., *Journal of a Residence on a Georgian Plantation in 1838–1839 by Frances Anne Kemble* (New York: New American Library, 1975).

Julia Floyd Smith, *Slavery and Rice Culture in Low Country Georgia, 1750–1860* (Knoxville: University of Tennessee, 1985).

Lorenzo D. Turner, *Africanisms in the Gullah Dialect* (1949; reprinted Ann Arbor: University of Michigan Press, 1974). Neither Turner nor Ian F. Hancock, "Gullah and Barbadian—Origins and Relationships," *American Speech* (Spring 1980), gives much attention to Fula sources of Gullah, though Hancock does note Gullah numerals in Fulfulde (p. 29). Perhaps there is an untapped linguistic vein here.

Ivor Wilks, "Salih Bilali of Massina," in *Africa Remembered*, ed. Philip D. Curtin. (Madison: University of Wisconsin Press, 1967), 145–151.

6

Lamine Kebe, Educator

In 1834, after nearly forty years of slavery in at least three Southern states, an old man whose slave name was "Paul" was magnanimously liberated by his last Christian master. Like the freeing of Abd ar-Rahman six years earlier, however, this gesture included neither economic nor American freedom. Needing and wanting to find a way home, "Paul" was forced to join with members of the American Colonization Society (ACS) dedicated to sending free blacks to the one part of Africa they knew anything about: Liberia, that semisettled coast about five hundred miles away from Kebe's actual homeland.

If this sequence of events had not occurred, it is likely that nothing would have been recorded about this man and his educational experiences in Africa and that he would not have become the stimulus for a significant campaign to send Christian literature in Arabic into West Africa. Nor is it likely that he would have gained passage back to Africa. But "Old Paul," as he was called in America, who was apparently called Lamine Kebe in Africa, did become known for a while among New York colonizationists and missionaries. He deserved even greater fame.

Kebe was quoted in Chapter 1 as saying, "There are good men in America, but all are very ignorant of Africa." He might have added "and of Islam." Little may be discovered to argue against either conclusion, but more may be found on the African who made the comment. A white American, Theodore Dwight, Jr., declared after several interviews in 1835 that Lamine Kebe was—like so many Africans in America—an excellent but untapped source of information about Africa. He also found Kebe to be an exemplary teacher and published some of his advice in *The American Annals of Education and Instruction*, making Kebe the only African quoted at length in a contemporary American professional journal. That Dwight also found in Kebe a stimulus for a plan to distribute Arabic-language Bibles in West Africa to advance Christianity there is ironic because Lamine Kebe's history is another reminder of how powerful the African culture and religion of Islam was even to a man who had been exiled for thirty or forty years and who had seen New York City and met good and helpful Christians. Kebe, in fact, chose to return to the land and religion he had been born to.

The earliest documented notices refer to introductions of "Old Paul" at two meetings in New York City late in 1834. He played a part in a carefully organized defense of the creation of a new settlement of former American slaves in Africa by a combined New York and Philadelphia company acting independently of the near-bankrupt parent American Colonization Society. One mention appeared in the ACS journal *The African Repository*:

> There was then in the room a venerable old man, who would present himself before them. His name in English was Paul, the aged. He had been thirty years in slavery, and was now free, and hoped once more to revisit his native land, and meet his family, from whom he had been so long separated. After being for so long a period a slave, he had at last met a Christian Master who set him free. . . .
>
> The old man . . . was a scholar, and could write in the Arabic, and knew the Bible in his own language, though he was ignorant that the art of printing had ever been invented. He had left behind him a wife and three children, and it was the earnest wish of the Society to send him home as soon as possible, in the hope that he might once more meet his family, before they parted, never more to meet in this world.
>
> The old man was then brought forward and related in broken English, the principal events of his life. He was of an affluent if not a noble family, and went 900 miles to an institution to acquire an education. After that he taught a school for five years. He was then married, and at a subsequent period went to Timbuctoo to obtain paper. On his way back he was surrounded when asleep, and awoke to the act of his captors putting fetters upon him. He was then taken down to a slave ship and brought to this country. He ended his narrative by stating his travels and transfer from master to master for the last 30 years . . . and concluded by invoking a blessing on this country.

In other words, after thirty years—possibly forty, as an 1864 Dwight report "Condition and Character of Negroes in Africa" suggests—of American slavery under several masters, following an African kidnapping (more likely from near Timbo than Timbuktu), marriage and children, and an academic history that suggests he was about thirty when taken away, a Christian master decided that "Paul, the aged" deserved to be freed. Neither this 1834 reporter nor Dwight chose to delve into "Paul's" trials as a slave among Christians. If they had, they might have found some reasons why he had not chosen to learn the language of his several purchasers and spoke only "broken English." As Dwight's subsequent interviews suggest, this man had the ability to learn English and he undoubtedly tried his best once he found listeners who might do him some good. The reporter also skipped over much that might have been informative about Africa, noting only that "Paul" spoke about his family; education; teaching; attempt to buy that rare commodity, paper; and capture—all without elaboration, and with no discussion, it may be noted, of any Muslim connections. Finally, "Paul" closed with a blessing on America. Very politic. There is no indication, however, that he received any personal assistance from this meeting.

A few months later "Paul" tried again. He decided—or agreed with an adviser—that his audiences might be more generous if he offered the good Christians something valuable in return for their aid. He knew he had to persuade his audiences that he was worthy of their assistance. Although the man is not named, surely the reference in the following paragraph about a mid-May 1835 meeting found in *The African Repository* six months after the meeting described earlier is "Paul" adding his new incentive:

> "A coloured man was now presented to the audience, who expected shortly to go out as an emigrant to Liberia. The gentleman who presented him said that he was an educated man, that he spoke, read, and wrote the Arabic language very perfectly; and was a professed believer in Christ. He intended to act as a missionary to his race. He had been liberated by his master for this end; and had been waiting now for 90 days for an opportunity of going."

This new Christian missionary message was helpful to "Paul's" sponsors; the New Yorkers raised $2,000 to help send emigrants to Liberia. Still, this report does not say whether "Paul" was one of them. Perhaps his audience had not been convinced by his sudden conversion. Oddly, two later mentions of "Paul" are also inconclusive about his returning. The secretary of the American

Colonization Society, Ralph R. Gurley, who appeared earlier in Chapters 2 and 4, wrote two years later, in 1837, that "Paul" had corresponded in Arabic with Umar ibn Said (see Chapter 7) while "preparing to embark at New York for Liberia." "Paul's" most important and most exasperating memorialist, Dwight, wrote that "Paul" "spent about a year in New York, under the care of the Colonization Society, while waiting for his ship to go out." But neither writer closed Kebe's American history.

Happily, another source suggests that "Paul" succeeded. A list of immigrants who arrived in Liberia on the ship *Indiana* August 19, 1835, includes a peculiarly named "Paul A. Mandingo" (Kebe's mother was a "Manenca" or Mandingo), freeborn, literate, age sixty, from "North Georgia." The name and data fit the man. Following this name is a pleasant addition that declares that this "Paul" moved on to Sierra Leone, which was closer to Kebe's actual homeland.

The most important source indicates that it is unlikely that "Old Paul" brought Christianity home with him. The one American who came to know him best, Dwight, was interested in distant people; familiar with seven or eight languages; a founder of the American Ethnological Society; and the editor of several magazines including his own *Dwight's American Magazine*. The offspring of one of the famous Connecticut Wits, Dwight (1796–1866) graduated from Yale in 1814, wrote travel books on Italy (1824) and northern Europe (1841), and, as a Free-Soiler against the spread of slavery wrote *The Kansas Wars* (1859). He was also a member of the New York Colonization Society and may have met Kebe at one of the meetings described earlier. He had clearly been impressed by this freeman, whose African name Dwight heard as "Lamen Kebe" or "Lahmen Kibby."

Dwight composed at least four essays about Kebe. Until very recently, however, it appeared that only two were published. Late in 1995, corrected galley sheets were found for a preface and some notes for a lengthy narrative on Kebe. Unfortunately, the middle sheets have not been found. The "Preface," however, includes Dwight's single description of Kebe: "about six feet high, well formed, of mild and grave countenance, friendly disposition, and dignified but simple demeanor." Dwight also concluded, no matter what Kebe told Christian New Yorkers, that Kebe was sincerely and wholly Muslim.

Kebe was also worth quoting. In an 1864 article, Dwight wrote that he had "held numerous and prolonged interviews" with Kebe, who was "deeply interested" in having "his communications concerning his native country and people, as well as his own history . . . published, for the information of Americans." But

Dwight's known publications shed light on only a small part of the information Kebe gave him. An exasperating list is offered by Dwight of information he had gathered from Kebe: "His accounts of [other African nations he had visited] abound in details of great novelty and interest. The same may be said of his communications on the history, customs, arts, religions, learning, languages, books, schools, teachers, travelers, productions, trade, of the mixed people among whom he lived."

And Kebe knew how to write history and ethnography: "Write down what I tell you exactly as I say it, and be careful to distinguish between what I have seen and what I have only heard other people speak of. They may have made some mistakes; but if you put down exactly what I say, by and by, when good men go to Africa, they will say, Paul told the truth." One wishes, then, Dwight had produced more.

But the two extant articles begin to enlighten. The first, in *The American Annals of Education and Instruction* (a very safe place politically), is underdeveloped and terminologically inconsistent, but it does supply essential information for tracking the early history of this individual and his scholarly clan.

> Lamen Kebe, (for that is his real name,) [probably Lamine—Mande for Arabic *Abd al-Amin,* Kebe—Serahule pronunciation, as I have been recently informed, for a branch of a teaching clan more fully described later] was born in the kingdom of Futa Jalloo, and travelled sufficiently during his youth to give much interest to the accounts he communicates. He performed two journeys, when quite young, to the Jaliba or Niger river, in one instance in company with an army of Mahomedans, in a successful war upon an idolatrous nation, to convert them to Islamism. His education, which commenced at fourteen [after seven years of learning the Quran by rote], and was finished at twenty-one, was obtained chiefly at Bunder, the city [not a city, but Bundu, homeland of Job Ben Solomon]. . . . He was a school-master five years in the city of Kebe [possibly the important Mande Muslim religious center Kebe, or Kaba to Mandingoes], which he left to travel to the coast [rather than to Timbuktu, as New Yorkers understood], to obtain paper for the use of his pupils, when he was taken and sold as a slave.

Kebe told Dwight several details about the African schools that were common in the Futa Jallon of Bilali Muhammad, Abd ar-Rahman, and Kebe. His schoolbooks were thirty manuscripts, a list dictated by Kebe but not clearly recorded by Dwight, used in studies beyond the reading of the Quran. Kebe also indicated that "several native African languages were written in Arabic characters."

Dwight understood that Kebe was "of mixed extract; his father being a Serecule, and his mother of the Manenca nation." Kebe also told something of the spread of Islam via education and of the movement of his anti-military teaching clan, the Jakhanke, from east of the middle Senegal River to Futa Jallon.

Dwight then apologized about not having enough space to pass on details "concerning this nation, its traditions, manners, manufactures, schools, high schools, &c.," because he wanted to show his academic readers that Kebe's language and knowledge were worthy of attention, though unknown "as yet" to "the learned of Europe . . . even our latest geographers." Dwight was correct.

After some pertinent and impertinent criticism of those who lacked information about Africa while knowledgeable men like Kebe who might have enlightened them were despised as being only slaves, Dwight reported that Kebe mentioned both male and female teachers—including an influential aunt, unfortunately unnamed, "who was much more learned than himself, and eminent for her superior acquirements and for her skill in teaching." Dwight may have overstated the extent of learning opportunities for women, but in fact others, including the explorer Mungo Park and later Usman Dan Fodio, the Fulani Emir of Sokoto, offered similar evidence on female scholars, especially his daughter.

Kebe then went into detail on Serahule schools. They were provided by the government and were, like some schools in other religions, divided according to sex. Kebe's remarks dealt with classroom procedure, student attendance, teacher attitudes, and bilingual education.

In some schools, boys and girls are under the care of the same master; but they are placed in separate rooms. Our informant had from fifty-five to fifty-seven pupils in his native town, after he had completed his education, among whom were four or five girls. His scholars, according to the plan pursued in his education, were seated on the floor, each upon a sheepskin, and with small boards held upon one knee, rubbed over with a whitish chalk or powder, on which they were made to write with pens made of reeds, and ink which they form with care, of various ingredients. The copy is set by the master by tracing the first words of the Koran with a dry reed, which removes the chalk where it touches. The young pupil follows these marks with ink, which is afterwards rubbed over with more chalk. They are called up three at a time to recite to the master, who takes the boards from them, makes them turn their backs to him, and repeat what they were to do the previous day, which they have a decided interest in doing to the best of their recollection; because it is the custom to mark every mistake with the stroke of a stick upon the shoulders.

The mind of our informant shows some of the traits of a professional school-master, and his opinions on pedagogy, claim some attention, as they are founded on experience, and independent of those current in other countries.

"It is of great importance," Lamen remarks, "that children should not be allowed to change school. In our country, no such thing is known or permitted, except when absolutely necessary. It is indeed permitted to a boy who has learnt all his master has to teach, to seek other teachers during the recess of his own school, if he does not neglect his own; and it is no uncommon thing for intelligent youth to attend the instructions of two or three teachers at different hours of the day. But it is very wrong to do as your children do in this country. When a boy has been punished, or for any other reason dislikes his teacher, you let him run all about to this school and that, and he learns nothing, and is good for nothing.

"You should be very careful too what kind of a teacher you get for your child. He must not be too severe, because the boy will be looking out all the while for a whipping, and cannot study; and he should not be an easy man, because if children have their own way, they will not study; you never knew one that would. An easy man will let them have their own way, and therefore they never will learn. But you should get a middle man for a schoolmaster. He will not frighten the boys all the time so that they cannot study; but yet he can speak to them now and then as if he would eat them up; and they will not forget it for months."

It is interesting to the friends of education in America, to hear of improvements introduced in the schools of other countries. Lamen Kebe has a high opinion of a certain process practised in some of the institutions of his native land, which he calls doubling; while of those in which it is not practised, he speaks with comparative contempt. In schools of the latter and common class, the Koran is taught in Arabic alone, which not being the vulgar language of any of the negroes, is totally unintelligible. In those in which the important process of doubling is adopted, the meaning of the Arabic words is explained as well as translated. He inquires with some interest, whether the doubling or explaining [bilingual] system is properly cultivated in the United States.

This article concluded with Dwight's attempt to record a Serahule vocabulary and to list texts known to Kebe. Dwight's vocabulary is a haphazard selection of nouns, adjectives, prepositions, and only three verbs, altogether about one hundred lexical items—of which fourteen are Arabic. When compared with two Serahule vocabularies Dwight mentions, his does not fare badly, though it is poorly printed. Fourteen words may be found in the original edition of Mungo Park's *Travels in the Interior Districts of Africa in 1795, 1796, and 1797*. Nineteen words may also be found in Sigismund Koelle's wonderful *Polyglotta Africana*, first published in 1854, which bears the descriptive subtitle *A Comparative Vocabulary of Nearly 300 Words and Phrases, in More Than 100 Distinct African Languages*.

Kebe's words for America are interesting: "alkitabiatu (a book country)"; sea, "Francos (bitter river)"; "black people's country—serambine diamau [diamani]." Dwight tried to list Kebe's books, handwritten in the absence of any press, and thought he was giving titles and leaving out long names of authors. He heard this: "Nahayi, Fakihu, Sani, Lauan, Taurat, (the Torah, or law of Moses,) Yabury, and Alsara, (parts of the Scriptures,) Ankidutilmamy, Segudin, Bunamara-kibura, Bunamara-wussita, Bunamara-fusilun, Sulaimy-kubura, Sanisy-kubura, Sanisy-wussita, Sanisy-sugura, Sanisy-suku, Aluwatriet, Bonomahha-jabby, Almahhama, and Talakiny."

Since I first offered, in 1984, translations of this list, which is important because it is instructive although little known and is closely paralleled by lists from at least three of Kebe's contemporaries also included in my earlier book, further reading and some disagreements by Ronald Judy have led me to some conclusions probably of interest only to specialists.*

These manuscripts signify study far beyond the basic reading of the Quran. Kebe was referring to the major subjects taught by advanced scholars: Arabic grammar, law, moral guidance from the Prophet's example, and theology; it

---

* "Nahayi"—*nahw*, or grammar (citing Jack Goody and his version of a Fula list in *Literacy in Traditional Societies* [1968], 224); "Fakihu"—*fiqh*, or jurisprudence (laws for men); "Sani"—*sunna*, or traditions of the Prophet Muhammad; "Lauan"—*lughah*, or linguistics; "Taurat"—*tawhid*, or theology (the laws of God or Allah). The remainder are texts and authors. "Alsara" is possibly the *Risala* of Ibn Zaid, a popular treatise on law that may have been quoted by Bilali (Chapter 5). "Bunamara-kibura" through "Bunamara-fusilun" indicates a multivolume or manuscript work by a single author. These may be texts on the uses of magic squares, numbers, and names in charms or amulets—called *gris-gris* and *jujus* by Europeans—provided by presumably spiritually powerful Muslims to both believers and animists (Goody, *Literacy in Traditional Societies*, 226). Another series by Sanusi follows. An as-Sanusi produced five volumes of religious commentary (according to Lamin Sanneh, who has studied Serahule traders, *The Jakhanke*, 99), and was

includes two commentaries on language, two on Islamic laws, four on theology, and one anthology of poetry.

Judy has argued that Kebe's pedagogy undermines the so-called universal categories of understanding of the Enlightenment philosophers who influenced so much of the West's misunderstanding of Africa and Africans. His is a heavy argument, but it is surely true that the admitted lack of experience of David Hume, Immanuel Kant, and G.W. F. Hegel, in particular, and Europeans and Americans, in general, in conversing with Africans as equals and in reading African manuscripts or understanding music, dance, religion, and other cultural signs must have kept them "ignorant of Africa," as Kebe correctly concluded.

Dwight's second essay, "Condition and Character of Negroes in Africa" (1864), is much more pretentious and much less satisfying. He began with a healthy denunciation of scholars of his time and place for having been so little interested in Africa and those Africans who had been brought to America by force and trickery. He went on to name available sources of information, "[Baptist missionary Thomas J.] Bowen [1857], [missionary David] Livingstone [1857], and [explorer Heinrich] Barth [1858]," for rectifying such a lapse in intelligence; denounced Catholicism as anti-literate; exaggerated the extent to which literacy using Arabic characters had spread across West Africa; imagined the lines of this spread as channels prepared and hungering for Protestant Christian influence and education; and then returned to the theme that a number of Africans in America were unconscionably treated "like beasts of the field" despite their being "men of learning and pure and exalted characters." He then named a few of these men—all presented in this book: "Job-Ben-Solomon," "Abder-rahman," "Omar-ben-Sayeed," and "Lahmen Kibby."

Dwight reasserted that he possessed voluminous notes gathered from Kebe. It is a great disappointment, however, that the rest of the essay includes only a few of these notes in what turns out to be an interesting but too wide-rang-

a scholar of *tawhid* and author of *Kubra*—Dwight's "Sulaimy-kubura" (Trimingham, *History of Islam in West Africa*, 81–82)? Probably as-Sanusi's *Aqidat Sughra* is the "Sanisy-sugura" later in Dwight's list. Dwight's "Aluwatriet" is close to "Watirati," an item in a contemporary African manuscript list he appended to an article by an African teacher called Kabwee. In turn, both are close to *Al-Witriyat*, the anthology of six poets mentioned by Goody as part of the advanced coursework among the Fulbe (*Literacy in Traditional Societies*, 225).

The multilingual—including Arabic—cultural theorist Ronald A.T. Judy has also commented on this list. Judy finds a grammar by al-Jurrumiya in "Yabury," another text by as-Sanusi in Dwight's "Ankidutilmamy," at-Tawankali's commentary on *fiqh* in "Talakiny,"and an al-Mukhtar text on Sufi law in Dwight's "Almahhama." The first three may be correct, but the last seems to me more likely to be the Maqamat of al-Hariri on grammar (Trimingham, 82).

ing survey of African Muslim intellectual acquirements in Africa that might be utilized by Christian missionaries. So far, as I mentioned earlier, only a galley-page-and-a-half "Preface" and three galley pages of notes have been found of Dwight's third effort.

My own investigations following Dwight's available leads corroborate all of his main points. Kebe undoubtedly came from a famous clan of pragmatic, dedicated Muslim teacher-priests in Africa. Kebe said his father was a Serahule—the founders of ancient Ghana, who were among the earliest converts to Islam south of the Sahara—and who were a very black people—and his mother a "Manenca" (Mande or Mandingo).

The still important town of Kaba (sometimes Kebe, Kangaba, and Kaniaba) was founded by Serahule or Jakhanke immigrants led by religious leaders from the Kaba or Kebe family of the Qadiriya brotherhood in the late 1770s. This group of itinerant teachers emphasized "faithfulness to the record" and memorization of important occurrences and history. Furthermore, this group sensibly combined, as a modern scholar who shares Kebe's first name, Lamin O. Sanneh, puts it, "local resources and outside inspiration." While constantly bringing young people to a deeper understanding of Islam by teaching the Quran in local languages as well as Arabic, it also utilized native religions and social practices that were not in direct opposition to Quranic teaching. Sanneh argues that the practice of the Jakhanke showed the "indigenous character of clerical Islam in West Africa." The Jakhanke were pacifists, although they sometimes traveled with militant Muslims on *jihad*s. They were not opposed to slavery. The Scottish explorer Mungo Park joined a coffle of enslaved captives en route to the coast that was led by reliable and very strong Serahule "slatees," as he called them, who were necessarily well informed about the lands and peoples they traveled among.

There should be little doubt about Kebe's geographical origins or about his family. He said he was from an affluent family, and he knew its history. Accordingly, there seems little reason to distrust the remainder of the information found in Dwight's writings. As is suggested earlier, however, there is too little information on Kebe personally. Instead, Dwight expanded on his own hobby of finding intelligent, literate Africans for his obvious purpose. He told of procuring Umar's autobiography, in Arabic, and a translation that he added to his second article—a gift from Kebe, actually, from correspondence in Arabic between Kebe and Umar. But Kebe's side of this correspondence has not yet been found. Dwight was, of course, pleased to report his understanding that Umar had converted to Christianity and had advised Kebe to do the same.

Toward the close of the 1864 article, Dwight quoted from a translation of Umar's "Life," an African-produced manuscript in Arabic, and he appended yet another in facsimile with a translation to help make his case about the utility of Arabic in spreading Christianity. In recently recovered papers (1995) mentioned earlier, now owned by Derrick Joshua Beard who generously showed them to me, the original Arabic manuscripts and translations of each of these documents have been found, along with translations of a prayer and of three amulets (short prayers to be worn in leather pouches around the neck); an amulet written in the form of a circle and a translation finding in it a prayer seeking protection for a trading enterprise—both written in Africa; and three letters (four pages) from the 1850s in Arabic from a Sana or Sawa See (Sonni Ali?) enslaved in South Carolina and Panama, accompanied by hesitant translations. These letters give minimal information about Sana See but do show his adherence to Islam. This lot of papers also shows that further documentation may yet be found on any of the people mentioned in this book.

From such evidence of literate Africans in America and the Liberian hinterland, Dwight was led to believe that Bibles would be welcome in Muslim West Africa. In the papers mentioned above there are originals or copies of eleven letters to Dwight on his campaign to send new and improved, that is, more eloquent than an 1811 translation of the Bible to West Africa. Eventually, late in the 1860s, Daniel Bliss, president of the Syria Protestant College and one of Dwight's correspondents, sent a case of Bibles in Arabic to Liberia to be distributed in its hinterland. This act paralleled the innovative Arabic studies program of the College of Liberia, founded by the important black St. Lucian Edward W. Blyden, who often visited the United States and Europe on behalf of his country and who became one of the most prominent Christians to write positively about African Muslims in the nineteenth century. One wonders what Lamine Kebe might have thought about his part in the campaign.

SELECTED READINGS

Edward Wilmot Blyden, *Christianity, Islam and the Negro Race* (1888) (reprinted Baltimore: Black Classic Press, 1994).

Theodore Dwight, Jr., "Condition and Character of Negroes in Africa," *Methodist Quarterly Reviw* (Jan. 1864), 77–90; and "Remarks on the Sereculehs, an African Nation, Accompanied by a Vocabulary of their Language," *American Annals of Education and Instruction*, V (1835), 451–456.

Jack Goody, *Literacy in Traditional Societies* (Cambridge: Cambridge University Press, 1968).

Ronald A. T. Judy, *(Dis)Forming the American Canon: African-Arabic Slave Narratives and the Vernacular* (Minneapolis: University of Minnesota Press, 1993).

Cheikh Hamidou Kane, *Ambiguous Adventure* (New York: Collier, 1969).

Mungo Park, *Travels in the Interior Districts of Africa in 1795, 1796, and 1797* (London: African Society, 1799).

George E. Post, "Arabic-Speaking Negro Mohammedans in Africa," *Missionary Herald* (April 1869), 114–117.

Lamin O. Sanneh, *The Jakhanke: The History of an Islamic Clerical People of the Sene-Gambia* (London: International African Institute, 1979).

J. Spencer Trimingham, *A History of Islam in West Africa* (London: Oxford University, 1962).

Fig. 21. Umar ibn Said, Photograph from a Daguerreotype, 1850s or 1860s, Davidson College Library, Davidson, North Carolina.

7

Umar ibn Said's Legend(s), Life, and Letters

The dignified Abd ar-Rahman and his dramatic story were famous for a year and have been recalled often since. The also dignified, less dramatic, proudly mysterious, even controversial Umar ibn Said and his varied writings were also the objects of attention, from 1819 to 1864—nearly all of Umar's American lifetime—and also into our own time. His Bible in Arabic, a daguerreotype portrait, and fourteen manuscripts in Arabic by Umar have been preserved. These include the only extant autobiography by an American slave in Arabic—a very legible, sixteen-page manuscript. (Abu Bakr as-Siddiq wrote another such autobiography but in Jamaica.) Umar's "Life" was thought to be lost after 1925 but was found late in 1995. Umar's grave has also been rediscovered. There is some debate over the religion of his life and his spirit. Once acclaimed as a convert to Christianity, as an Arabian who found no fault with American slavery and who despised Africans, Umar has recently been more closely examined as a closet Muslim, religiously conservative as his people, the Fulbe—clearly African—regularly were. Today, a Quranic school, or *masjid*, in Fayetteville, North Carolina, has been named after Al Hajj Umar ibn Said. In the past, interest in Umar was mostly regional, restricted to the Carolinas, where he lived. About thirty-five articles, including mixes of fact and fiction, surfaced by the 1970s; the numbers have risen since then and are likely to continue to do so because Umar has become a significant element in the ancient struggle between Christian and Muslim scholars, propagandists, and wishful thinkers; between fact and fiction regarding American and Christian slavery and the humanity and intelligence of Africans.

Despite authoritative sources, including letters in his own hand, on Umar's life, legends fostered by white Christian romantic, racist, and religious writers predominated over the years, beginning about 1825. Into the 1980s, this romantic Southern, antiblack, militant Christian legend grew over and around what was known about the man. Fitting the earlier representation, Umar's Arabic Bible, a gift of Christians interested in his conversion or his salvation, has been preserved, whereas an earlier gift, a Quran in English, has not. With some variations over time, this legend represents Umar as a well-educated Arabian prince who somehow found himself in Africa, being captured by Africans, whom, the tale declares, he despised all his life. There is some confusion here with Joel Chandler Harris's fictional Ben Ali (Chapter 5) and perhaps Abd ar-Rahman (Chapter 4). The hero of this legend was in no way African. He had straight hair, a light complexion, and the "features and the form of an Apollo Belvidere"—the Greek sculpture raised as an ideal of European, and therefore universal, manly beauty. His capture by "constantly warring" Africans led to his being sold and shipped to Charleston, South Carolina. There he ran away, not from a master—for in this legend, all slaveholders were kind—but from his second master's overseer, who, as sometimes happened, was unkind. Umar was saved, however, by a one-time governor of North Carolina, John Owen, a full-time gentleman who recognized the royal quality in the strange runaway. In a few years, the good governor and some noble ministers of the Gospel sensitively turned Umar away from his early stubborn faith in the "bloodstained Koran" and toward a marvelously pious later career "worshipping at the feet of the Prince of Peace." He naturally had also been turned from any interest in Africa—perhaps because he had his own garden and horse and buggy, or possessions equally unusual for a slave—and toward a sincere love of white Americans and their offspring, to whom he told wonderful tales.

This is a sweet "before the war" Southern story. It is also a misrepresentation in several of its essential and often contradictory details. This legend was the product of a lengthy series of misrepresentations based on disrespectful attitudes toward Muslims and Africans. True religious sensibilities in a Muslim and literacy or "civilization" in an African were not easily admitted: the black man who believed in one god, who prayed, who knew biblical figures, and who could read and write had to be called an Arabian to be allowed in most ante- and postbellum Southern publications.

A glance at some of these works suggests how the legend grew. Early on—

as happened with other Africans, non-Muslim as well as Muslim—Umar's dignified, even proud, carriage and manners led visitors to see in him a prince. So argued one minister, G.T. Bedell, who may have witnessed Umar's baptism into the Presbyterian Church (recorded in 1821), in "Prince Moro" (1825). Following up on translations of an autobiography Umar wrote in 1831 and of two letters Umar wrote to Lamine Kebe, Ralph R. Gurley, secretary of the American Colonization Society, declared that Umar had completely converted to Christianity (1837). Both of these writers allowed Umar to be an African, but a decade later the legend began to take its ultimate shape. Umar was called "Monroe," a royal Arabian scholar, in an unsigned Wilmington, North Carolina, newspaper article in 1847; was seen as an Arabian prince who looked like a model Greek rather than an African and was saved by the governor from a bad overseer in "Prince Omeroh: Romantic Experience of a Princely Slave—A Strange Story of the Old Plantation Days," also unsigned in a Raleigh, North Carolina, newspaper, July 1884; was called by a pure Confederate propagandist a slave-trading Arabian Sheikh caught just above the *Congo River*! and brought by a *New England* ship to America, and purchased by good Governor Owen in "Meroh—A Slave" by another unnamed North Carolinian in 1887—my emphases; was three times misidentified as Governor Owen's slave and an Arabian in Louis T. Moore's "Prince of Arabia" (1927); was similarly misidentified in "The Story of Prince Omeroh: Native Arabian, [etc.]" by Calvin Leonard, 1934; and was proclaimed a literate prince and "not an African" by Margaret McMahon in "Bladen Slave Was Also a Prince" (1968).

In order to end up with such an antiblack and anti-Muslim legend, several earlier articles—and his portrait, the frontispiece in this chapter which is clearly that of an African—had to be overlooked. Not fitting were such pieces as the following. In an 1819 letter about Umar to Francis Scott Key, author of our national anthem, John Louis Taylor of Raleigh told Key that Umar might not mind being sent back to his homeland in Africa, where he would probably give a positive picture of America. This letter was accompanied by a two-page manuscript by Umar showing that he had been a Quranic scholar (see Figs. 22 and 23). The 1825 article mentioned earlier inadvertantly supplied a shrewd clue to an understanding of the man: Some enslaved Africans in North Carolina saw in Umar a "pray-god to the king," a *marabout*, or a kind of religious counselor to non-Muslim rulers. Umar's autobiography, first translated in 1848, clearly establishes his African homeland; education; literacy; early adherence to Islam; and, it seems, conversion to Christianity. There is a correction of the Arabian misidentification by an unnamed observer in a Raleigh newspaper article in

"An African Scholar" (1853) and a more significant article by Rev. Mathew B. Grier, the minister of the church Umar last attended, who admitted Umar's African origins and who also expressed some doubt about the absoluteness of his conversion to Christianity in "Uncle Moreau" (1854 and 1859).

Umar is called an ex-prince and a Freemason but visibly an African by John F. Foard recalling an 1855 visit with Umar in "A True Story of an African Prince in a Southern Home" (1904). Another visiting minister, William Plumer, remarked upon Umar's refined "whole person and gait" and Christian—why not Muslim?—character in "Meroh, A Native African" (1863). Umar was properly recognized as being from Senegal, Africa, and as being purchased by General rather than Governor Owen when much of his autobiography was first printed in translation in 1864 by Theodore Dwight, Jr., whom we met in Chapter 6. Umar is knowledgeably included in a transatlantic context in George Post's "Arabic-Speaking Negro Mohammedans in Africa" (1869). His autobiography was finally authoritatively translated and published in the *American Historical Review* (1925). His story was also accurately treated in "Omar ibn Said, a Slave Who Wrote an Autobiography in Arabic," published in the *Journal of Negro History* (1954). Another twelve articles offer further variations. Some are truer than others. All are included in my *African Muslims in Antebellum America* (1984).

Inconsistencies abound in many of the pieces unrelated to Umar's autobiography. The mix of sentimentality, ethnic wonderment, negrophobia, Christian presumptions, and carelessness in this legend needs sorting out. Muslim scholars have taken heart because of the equivocal conclusion about conversion expressed by Umar's last minister; their knowledge that Fula Muslims, in particular, have long stood out as being true to their religion; and evidence in all of the available Arabic writings by Umar found up to 1995. They may create their own legend—beginning with assuming that Umar made a pilgrimage to Mecca. This notion is not impossible, as many others did so from Senegal and Mali in his time, but is debatable—a matter to be taken up below. On the other hand, until modern scholars of both persuasions get to further study the original manuscript of Umar's autobiography, proof of its reported assertions—according to Christian translators—of his adopting Christianity will also have to be postponed. Undoubtedly, even examination of the manuscript will not finally settle the question.

It is evident that Umar was a spiritual soul who needed to pray regularly with others who prayed. He might have agreed to baptism in order to be allowed to do so and to enjoy a level of comfort and even prestige among Christian bookmen not available to other African-born servants. And he may have done so out of an appreciation for the genuine kindness of his ultimate purchaser James Owen and his family and for some aspects of Christianity. Others, including ar-Rahman, Kebe, King, and five African Jamaicans, also said that they admired elements of the Christian religion—but they all reverted at the first opportunity. None of these men, however, was reported to have declared a conversion as definitely as Umar. After setting the record as straight as possible on Umar's life, I will turn to his letters for further insights into this impressive African.

Umar's actual life, or what is known of it from the better pieces cited previously—and his autobiography—goes something like this. He was not an Arabian but an African, a dark Tukolor Fula, probably kin, at some remove, to Job, Yarrow Mamout, Abd ar-Rahman, Charno, Bilali, and Salih Bilali. His portrait clearly reflects contemporary descriptions of his color, hair, and physiognomy as being "distinctly of the African character," as Rev. Bedell wrote. He was born around 1765 in Futa Toro (present-day Senegal—see Map 1) to a father who had six sons and five daughters and a mother, whom he regularly commemorated in his American-Arabic writings, who had three sons and one daughter. At age five, when his father was killed in a war, he was taken by an uncle to be raised and was educated by an older brother and others in Futa Toro, Bundu (Job's country), and possibly in Futa Jallon. Three of his teachers are named in his autobiography, but no Fulbe family or clan name is given. His most important activities in Africa—judging by the space he gave them in his autobiography—were his training in and practicing of the Five Pillars of Islam: the Quranic obligations on praying five times a day, fasting, giving alms to the poor, fighting for the faith, and going on pilgrimages. One translation has him going to Mecca; another appears to refer to burial sites of local saints. (Recently, Muslim enthusiasts have added "Al Hajj" to Umar's name because, apparently, he said he had gone to Mecca. Although there are records establishing that many Muslims from Senegal did go to Mecca around 1800, there must have been some exaggeration in Umar's case. His pilgrimage would have been remembered in his homeland, and he would undoubtedly have talked about so wonderful a journey when he was in America.) Finally, of course, Umar declared his belief in one god and his prophet, Muhammad. Apparently, however, Umar did not have a family of his own in either Africa or America. No one mentions a wife or children—practically, socially, and religiously an obligation on either continent and in either religion.

Umar had not been a prince but had come from some wealth, as he appears to have told an American that his father had seventy slaves. According to his own account, he had been a scholar for twenty-five years; a teacher; and then, according to his minister, a trader in "salt, clothes, &c." This etcetera may or may not have included slaves. Some African-born slaves in America saw in Umar a "pray-god to the king," an adviser to a non-Muslim court. There may have been some mistake on his part that led to his capture and exile, but he was also a soldier against the infidels. Umar first told of being captured in a war, probably against the anti-Muslim Bambaras from Kaarta to the northeast or from Massina to the southeast who defeated the Almaamy of Futa Toro just north of Bure around 1807, the year Umar was sent to America. He was taken captive in that country, he said, by a large army.

In a beautifully written 1819 manuscript, Umar said he wanted to be seen again at Kaba or Kebe (see Chapter 6—a cultural center of the Mandingo Muslim people) in Bure, suggesting that this city was his home at the time of his capture. The accompanying letter from Taylor to Francis Scott Key suggested that Umar might be willing to return—perhaps as a Christian missionary. Shortly thereafter, however, Umar began to change his mind and story. He thought it might not be good to return because his friends might be dead or dispersed. Then, as Umar grew older in America, he seems to have catered to an American need for dark impressions of Africa. Interviewers reported that he acted as if something too terrible to talk about had happened in Bure and as if he would not want to go home again. This attitude contrasts markedly with impressions given by Abd ar-Rahman and Lamine Kebe, who offered much brighter pictures of the "Dark Continent." Of course, these two were being helped to go home.

Other African adults, such as Abd ar-Rahman, had suffered humiliations similar to Umar's. Umar was led to what he called the "great sea" and to a ship that took a month and a half to carry him to Charleston, South Carolina, the chief slave port in the South. He said that there were only two others on the ship who shared his language. The "large army" had apparently sent off more than Fulbe enemies—possibly the others were of the people whom Umar had been advising.

The American landing brought Umar a good first master, but he died. Umar's second master was not religious and demanded heavy physical labor. Umar would not stand for those conditions. He ran for about thirty days until he was taken out of a Fayetteville, North Carolina, church where he had gone to pray and was put in a prison. There his mild, well-mannered, and dignified ways and his writing on the walls attracted local attention. After somehow getting an evil sort of purchaser out of the way around 1811, James Owen, a one-time local militia officer (thereby earning the title of General), took Umar into his home.

According to all accounts, General Owen and his brother, Governor John Owen (1828–1830), treated Umar as the frail, spiritual, soon-to-die exotic that Umar said he was and required little from him. The poor slave, then around forty, hung on for the next fifty-three years. The General was so good that he managed to find a Quran in English at Umar's request and had it read to the near satisfaction of his scholarly slave. Umar reportedly maintained his required fasts and dietary rules for some time, and he seems not to have tried to master the language of the New World. One visitor thought he had never heard such bad "broken English." Perhaps Umar had come to America too late, but it might also be that, like other Muslim slaves among a few friends but many enemies, he saw little gain in trying to learn a new language.

Like Abd ar-Rahman, Umar attended church. Presbyterians were serious prayers, as he was. In 1821 he became a church member and was baptized. His Arabic Bible was used so much that it had to be recovered, apparently more than once. There is no evidence thus far, however, that Umar ever attempted to copy more than two pieces (the Lord's Prayer and the Twenty-third Psalm) from it. Several visitors to Fayetteville and to Owen's other home in Wilmington asserted that Umar was a wonderful Christian. Several ministers mentioned uplifting moral and spiritual conversations with Umar. Within his lifetime, he seems to have talked with adults rather than with the children described as listening to his stories by the African-disparaging myth mentioned before. His last minister, Rev. Mathew B. Grier, liked to think Umar was a mature Christian but allowed a little doubt as he hedged and wrote that "by all outward signs" Umar seemed to be a "sincere believer in Jesus Christ." As I indicated before, this equivocation offered an opening for Muslims to have their own ideas about Umar's religious beliefs.

Creators of legends and would-be biographers of Umar have an enormous advantage over those seeking the truth about others discussed in this book because Umar was encouraged to write over and over again in Arabic and was urged to write more than a few lines. This cannot be said for most of those considered in this book. So Umar often wrote; he wrote for people who could not read his language and who accepted Umar's characterization of the contents no matter what his subject matter actually was. He also undoubtedly wrote for himself, to maintain his faith through rewriting the words of Allah or God.

There are fourteen extant available productions of his hand; eleven, avoiding duplication, are reproduced here. There are mentions of eight others of which translations or paraphrases exist, although the original manuscripts have not been found. Unlike Abd ar-Rahman, who told contributors to his freedom fund that he was writing the Lord's Prayer in Arabic when he was actually writing the Fatiha, the opening chapter of the Quran, Umar usually actually wrote the Lord's Prayer—and he wrote it often. This was a sufficient sign to Christians that he was a convert. It may be argued, however, that nothing is said in that prayer that is peculiarly Christian. Sometimes Umar also seems to have let it be thought that he was writing the Lord's Prayer when he was only making a list of Owen family members, and his last supposed Lord's Prayer was actually a selection from the Quran. Umar also wrote the Twenty-third Psalm for visitors. Again, the psalm contains nothing that a Muslim might not be able to say in prayer to Allah.

One translator ruefully noted in 1904 in a note to his rendition of Umar's Twenty-third Psalm, written in 1855, "It is a little startling to find that 'Uncle Moro' still retained a little weakness for Mohammed." The supposedly Christian prayer was preceded by the traditional Muslim invocation to Allah and his Prophet Muhammad. This addition was Umar's regular practice. The notes in Umar's Bible and all extant manuscripts open with or include invocations to Allah and, usually, to his Prophet Muhammad; emphasize Umar's need of help; and recognize his responsibility to be strong in his faith.

But according to translators, Umar's autobiography and several currently unavailable translations make bold assertions of his giving up the Prophet Muhammad for the Prophet Jesus Christ. At least three documents—including, reportedly, two to "Paul," or Lamine Kebe—urge other Muslims to do so too. I will pass on those translations, but let us look first at facsimiles of Umar's available writings.

It is to be expected that the earliest known Umar manuscript, two beautifully written pages from 1819, Figs. 22 and 23, should be a melding of Hadith and Quranic excerpts. It is a sophisticated prayer for assistance by a man in forced exile. It begins with the Fatiha or first Surah of the Quran: "All praises to Allah, Who created all of us to worship Him. See what works they do; what they say; those who do good will have good; those who do evil will have evil." This is followed by "Greetings and peace to mindud [commander?] and John Owen and those with them of the community of Christians in the place called Rula [Raleigh?] from high to low; live! And to my brethren unreachable in a far country. I say then, as I begin: Blessed be He in Whose hands everything is owned, and all is capable."

Following are several lines of poetry based on the Hadith (traditions of the Prophet); Umar's arabesque; what appears to be a date transliterated from English ("November eighteen, Sunday, nineteen[?]"); *ayat*s, or verses, from

Surah 53.21–23a—against Christian idolatry—and Surah 2.285—significant because it implies that there are those who accept all apostles or prophets equally: "We make no distinction (they say) between one and another of His apostles."

Is there a rationale here for accepting Jesus as an apostle or prophet, as he is accepted elsewhere in the Quran (Surah 3.45)? This acceptance does not mean, of course, that Jesus is seen in the Quran as a savior or as God.

The following Surah, 2.286, declares that Allah does not demand too much but asks that Allah forgive believers in the land of unbelievers; Surahs 41.46 and 80.34–37 move toward the judgment all have to face, described more fully in 82.19 and 78.40. Umar's reference to his African home follows: "I am wanting you to know I want to be seen in a place called Africa in a place called Kaba in Bewir [Bure]." The manuscript closes with thirteen *ayats* from Surah 67 (al-Mulk), including lines on Allah's knowing a believer's mind even if the believer is not able to proclaim his thoughts openly.

John Louis Taylor, who sent this manuscript to Francis Scott Key, said he had other manuscripts by Umar, but these have not yet been found.

Umar wrote in Arabic in the Bible sent to him by Key. Inside the front cover are four inscriptions in Arabic; the first and fourth read, "All Praises to Allah, or God," the second, "All good is from Allah." The third is illegible. These expressions are Quranic; perhaps their origin does not exclude the possibility of their referring to the God of all peoples who could read. The only page annotated by Umar, the final one, begins similarly. It reads, "Praise God," then is illegible until halfway through Umar's third line, which appears to be a personal prayer he wrote often: "My name is Umaru, son of Sayyid; my mother is Umhan Yasnik. May God comfort her resting place" (Fig. 24).

Although Fig. 25 is identified as the Twenty-third Psalm by a handwritten note, the manuscript is actually the Lord's Prayer. This prayer, often recommended for new converts to Christianity, is preceded here by the curious statement, "And this is how you pray, you." Umar seems to be separating himself from Christians. This may have been written in 1828, as on its reverse is a transcription of a Victor Hugo poem with that date written beneath.

Also mismarked, Fig. 26 is not the Lord's Prayer but a list of nine James Owen family members following a design close to that found in Fig. 22. This may have been written in 1828 as it appears in the same scrapbook as Fig. 25.

The Fig. 27 and Fig. 28 manuscripts were found together in a notebook. It may have been written in 1840—the date given in Louis T. Moore's "Prince of Arabia" (1927), wherein Moore described the manuscript. It begins exactly

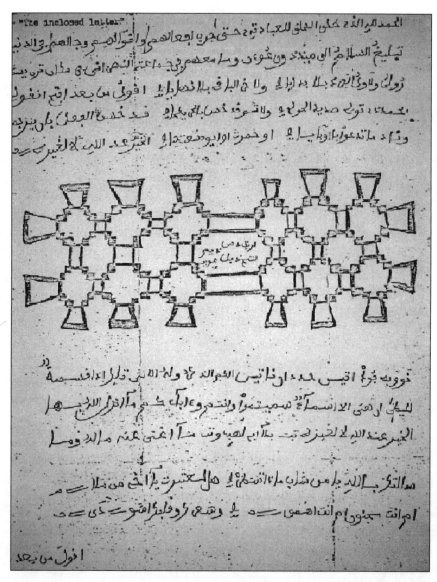

Figs. 22 & 23. The Earliest Known Ms. (two pages) by Umar, the "inclosed letter" from John Louis Taylor to Francis S. Key, 1819. Franklin Trask Library, Andover Newton Theological Seminary, Newton, Mass.

القول من بعد اقفيه القول بمحمد ﷺ توكل لنا يد الحول الجبر لمنذ الله ...
لغيره الا من الرسول بما انزل اليه من ربه والملائكة وكتبه وكتبه ورسله لا نفرق في
بين احد من رسله وقالوا سمعنا واستعنا غفرانك ربنا واليك المصير لا يكلف الله نفسا
الا وسعها لها ما كسبت وعليها ما اكتسبت ربنا لا تؤاخذنا ان نسينا او اخطأنا ربنا
لا تحمل علينا اصرا كما حملته على الذين من قبلنا ربنا ولا تحملنا ما لا طاقة لنا به
... بقول الله تعالى ومن عمل صالحا فلنفسه ... وعليها
سمعت بقول الله تعالى ومن قضى حاجة المسلم قضى الله له حاجته يوم يبعث الخلائق ...
اخيه وابيه وابنه وصاحبته وفصيله وبنيه ... منهم يومئذ سعى يغنيه ...
سمعت بقول الله عز وجل ومن قضى حاجة المومن قضى الله له حاجته يوما لا تضطرب فيه ...
... شيخا او ... من يوم بعثه الله بوم رمضان ... ساعدته بدا والله وبقول الشارع يا ابنتي
... إني أراك ان تجزي ... بطها ما يستحق ... حتى في مثل اليمن يستحق المجي
... بيعة السلام وهو علي كل شئ ... فهو يرجو هو الله خلق الموت والحياة ليبلوكم ...
الذي عمله وهو الرحمن بزالقهر الذي خلق سبع سموات ... ما تري في خلق رحمان من
تفاوت وما رجع البصر هل تري من فطور ثم ارجع البصر كرتين ينقلب اليك البصر خاسئا وهو
حسير ولقد زينا السماء الدنيا بمصابيح وجعلناها رجوما للشياطين واعتدنا لهم عذاب
السعير وللذين كفروا بربهم عذاب جهنم وبئس المصير اذا القوا فيها سمعوا
لها شهيقا وهي تفور تكاد تميز من الغيظ كلما القي فيها فوج سألهم خزنتها
الم ياتكم نذير قالوا بلي قد جاءنا نذير فكذبنا وقلنا ما نزل الله من شئ ان انتم
الا في ضلال كبير وقالوا لو كنا نسمع او نعقل ما كنا في اصحاب السعير
فاعترفوا بذنبهم فسحقا لاصحاب السعير ان الذين يخشون ربهم بالغيب لهم
مغفرة واجر كبير واسروا قولكم او اجهروا به انه عليم بذات الصدور وعلى

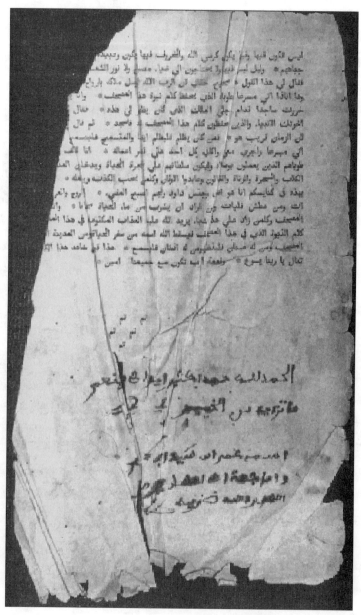

Fig. 24. Only Annotated Page (the final p. of Revelation) in Umar's Bible, Davidson College.

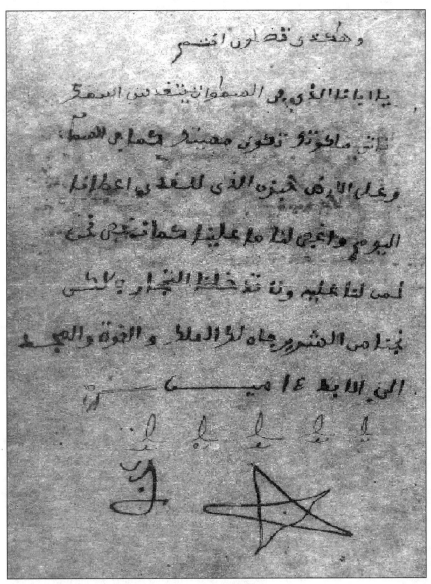

Fig. 25. Umar's Lord's Prayer (mismarked "23rd Psalm"), 1828? John Owen Papers, North Carolina State Archives, Raleigh.

Fig. 26. List of Owen Family Names (mismarked "The Lord's Prayer"), John Owen Papers, North Carolina State Archives, Raleigh.

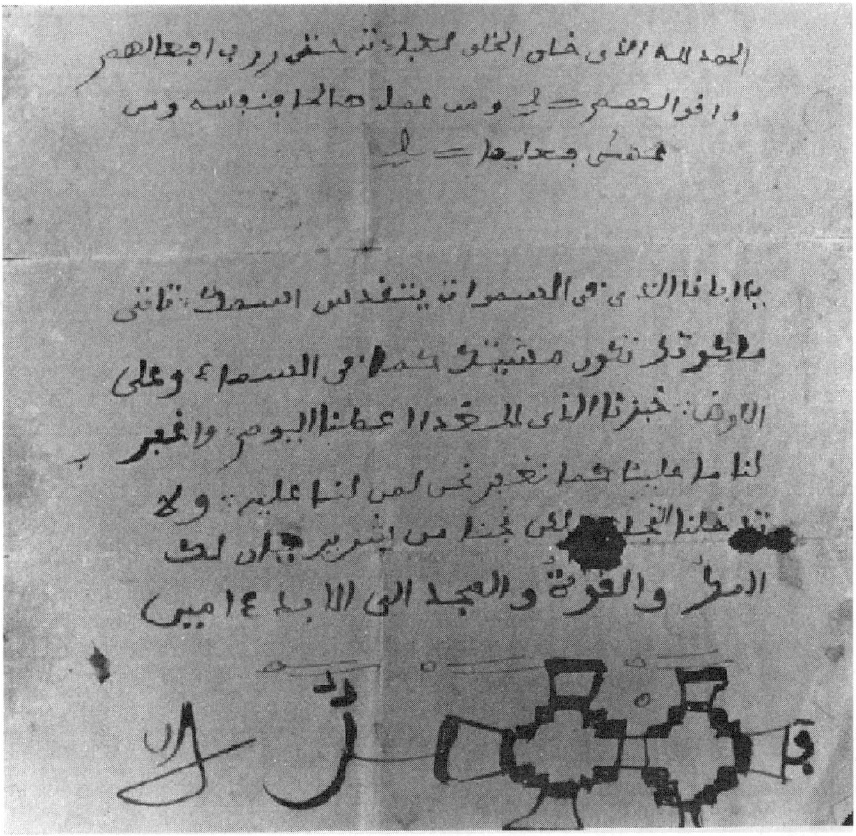

الحمد لله الذي ي خلق الخلو لجلا نت حتى رو ب اجعالهم

و اڧو الحصو = لي و من عمل هالحا ونواسه و من

عمى جعليها = لي

با ابا نا الذ ي ٯى السموا ت يتغدس اسمك ثاني

ملكو تك نكون مشيتك كما ٯى السما ء وعلى

الا رض: خبزنا الذ ى للغدا اعطنا اليوم وانغر

لنا ما علينا كما نغ ڧرنحن لمن انا علينا: ولا

ت خلنا التج بى لك لكن نجنا من اشر ير جان لك

الملك والقوة والمجد الى الا بد ا ١٤ ميں

Fig. 27. The Lord's Prayer, 1840?, Davidson College.

as does the Taylor manuscript with the Fatiha: "Thanks be to God, whom creatures were created to worship. He is the Lord of actions and sayings. Whomever does good, does so for himself; and whomever does evil will have evil." This is followed by The Lord's Prayer.

Another Lord's Prayer, Fig. 28, is preceded by the Bismillah, a conventional Muslim invocation: "In the name of God the Merciful, the compassionate. May God have mercy on the Prophet Mohammed." This is followed by Umar's benediction: "My name is Umaru, son of Sayyid; my mother is Umhan Yasnik. May God comfort her resting place."

In 1855 John F. Foard, another colonizationist, asked Umar for some of his writing. Umar sent him a manuscript that was translated by Princeton professor R. D. Wilson in 1904 (Fig. 29). It was the Twenty-third Psalm, preceded by the Bismillah: "In the name of God, the merciful and gracious. May god have mercy on the Prophet Mohammed." This led to Wilson's observation that "'Uncle Moro' still retained a little weakness for Mohammed." The translator could make nothing of the writing in the box, but it is Umar's benediction for his mother.

Fig. 30, an important manuscript, was given to the daughter of a prominent minister by James Owen in 1857. It was supposed to be the Lord's Prayer but is not from the Bible at all. Umar reached far back into his Quran to recall Surah 110. Suggestively, this was one of the last recitations from Allah—as Muhammad declared—before the death of the Prophet. Umar must have felt as if he were near a similar crisis. He also signed it: "My name is Umar."

Figs. 31, 32, and 33 show manuscripts that are undated. James Owen's daughter Eliza kept a scrapbook that included these three manuscripts. Fig. 31 includes the Bismillah, Umar's arabesque, and the names of Eliza and five other children.

Fig. 32 contains the Bismillah, the Twenty-third Psalm, and Quranic phrase "All good is from Allah, and no other." Umar signed his name in the star.

Fig. 33 is a provocative statement. The Bismillah is extended to praise the Creator and "the Lord of actions and sayings." But line 5 has been translated: "You recognize as a servant and son [of God?] Jesus." Does Umar not do so? Another line is not visible.

Thus far, it is surely possible to discern Umar the Muslim under Umar the Christian in these documents. But translators of presently unavailable Umar manuscripts—all Christian, of course—discovered a convert. Leaving aside Umar's "Life" for the moment, let us glance at some translated items. In 1835, Gurley ordered translations of two Umar letters to Kebe that supposedly urged the latter to "lay aside Mahomet's prayer and use the one which our blessed savior taught his disciples—'our Father, &c.' and god has been good to us in bringing us to this country and placing us in the hands of Christians. Let us now wake up and go to Christ, and he will give us light. God bless the American land! God bless the white people!"

This exhortation is so developed that it must appear that these were the words in Arabic. But it seems too pat and pleasing to be true. Umar did go on, according to this translation, and declared reason enough to be grateful: "My lot is at last a delightful one. From one man to another I went until I fell into the hands of a pious man. He read the Bible for me until my eyes were opened, now I can see; thank God for it. I am dealt with as a child, not as a servant."

Another missionary wrote that sometime around 1860, Umar's mistress gave the near centenarian a blank book for another autobiography. He filled it with Arabic writing. George E. Post, a missionary in Syria, saw the manuscript in 1868 and found "the pith of the scheme of redemption, in a series of Scripture passages from the Old and New Testaments." Post wrote that these passages were followed by an appeal to Umar's African relatives—who were not likely to ever see it: "Salaams to all who believe on the Lord Jesus Christ. I have given my soul to Jesus the Son of God. O, my countrymen [of] Bundah [Bundu], and Phootoor [Futa Toro], and Phootdalik [Futa Jallon?], . . . Come, come, come, come to Jesus the Son of God, and ye shall find rest to your souls in the day of judgment."

This excerpt would seem to settle the question about Umar's ultimate religious stance on the side of the Christians. But it is, once again, an invisible writing because the original manuscript has yet to be seen by modern scholars. In addition, Post's dating may be inaccurate. The manuscript may have been written before Umar wrote his Surah 110 around 1857.

Then there is Umar's "Life." In 1925, J. Franklin Jameson, then managing editor of the *American Historical Review,* authorized, intelligently introduced, and annotated a translation of Umar's most important writing, which Jameson titled "Autobiography of Omar ibn Said, Slave in North Carolina, 1831." He described the original document's history, its first translation in 1848 by Alexander I. Cotheal, "for many years . . . treasurer of the [American] Ethnological Society, and . . . a fancier of Arabic manuscripts." He recalled a second translator, Rev. Isaac Bird, a missionary in Syria from 1823 to 1835 whose effort some time later became the basis of the 1925 translation—and was probably the one quoted by Theodore Dwight, Jr., in Chapter 6—which was revised in the 1920s by Dr. R. M. Moussa, secretary of the Egyptian Legation in Washington.

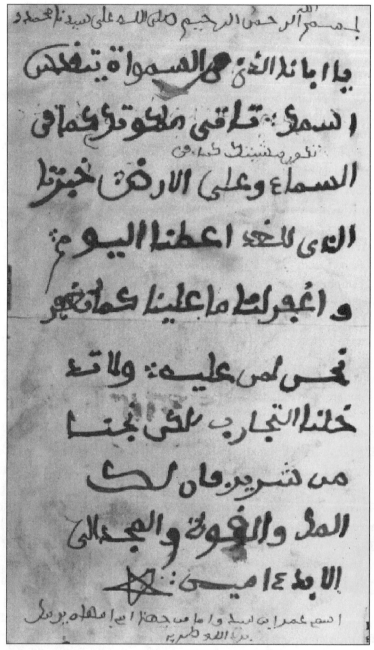

Fig. 28. The Lord's Prayer, signed by Umar, Davidson College.

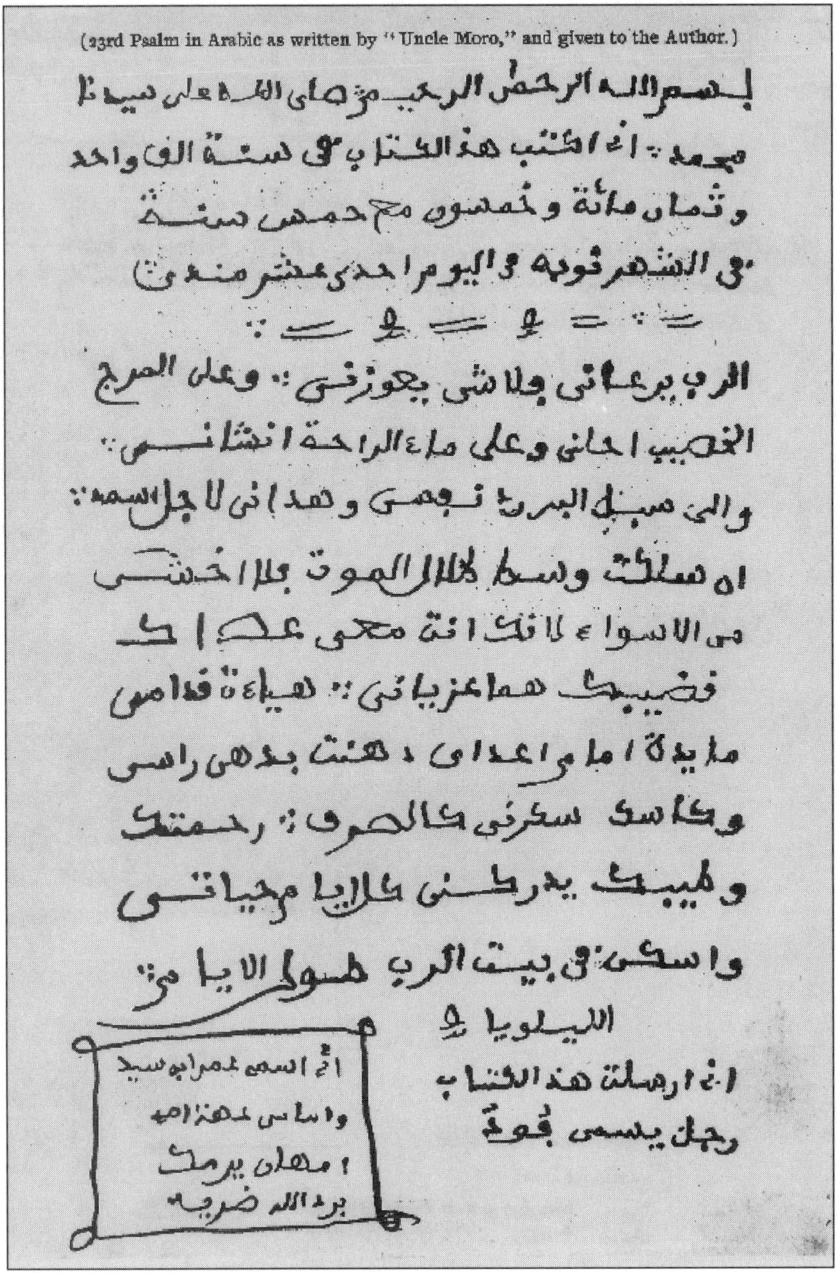

(23rd Psalm in Arabic as written by "Uncle Moro," and given to the Author.)

بسم الله الرحمن الرحيم صلى الله على سيدنا
محمد : انا اكتب هذا الكتاب في سنة الف واحد
وثمان مائة وخمسون مع خمس سنة
في الشهر فوبه و اليوم احدى عشر منه
الرب يرعاني فلا شي يعوزني : وعلى المرج
الخصيب احياني وعلى ماء الراحة انشأنس :
والى سبل البر يرجعني وهداني لاجل اسمه :
ان سلكت وسط ظلال الموت فلا اخشى
من الاسواء لانك انت معي عصاك
قضيبك هما عزياني : هيأت قدامي
مائدة امام اعداي : دهنت بدهن راسي
وكاسي سكرني كالصرف : رحمتك
وطيبك يدركني كل ايام حياتي
واسكن في بيت الرب طول الايام :
الليلويا
انا رسلت هذا الكتاب
رجل يسمى فورد

انا اسمي عمر ابو سيد
واساس بلدي
ا ماهل بيرمك
برد الله ضريحه

Fig. 29. The 23rd Psalm, 1855, John Frederick Foard, *North America and Africa: Their Past, Present and Future and Key to the Negro Problem*, 1904.

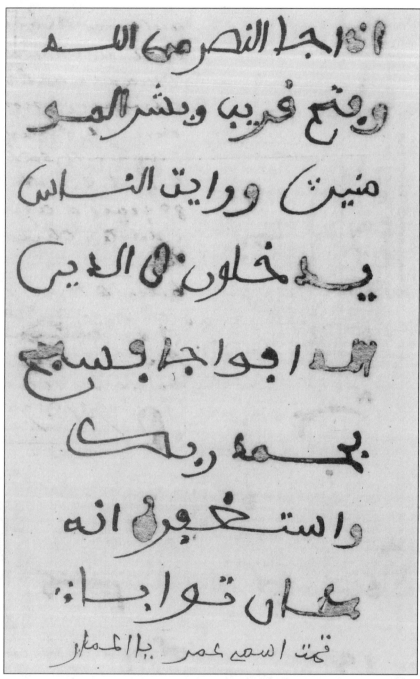

Fig. 30. Umar's Latest Known Extant Writing: Surah 110, 1857, University of North Carolina at Chapel Hill.

148

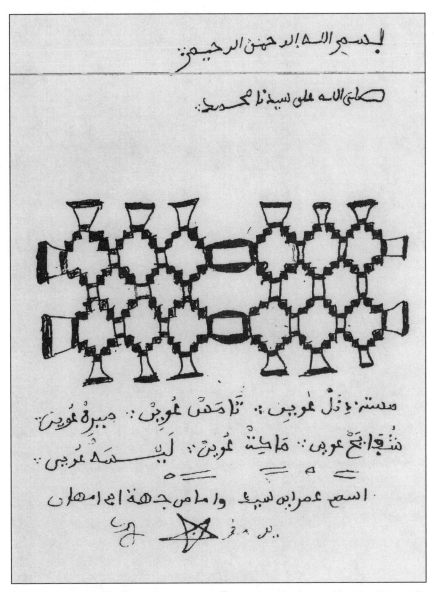

Fig. 31. List of Owen Family Names, Eliza H. Owen Scrapbook owned by Mrs. Trammell, Atlanta, photo courtesy of Thomas C. Parramore.

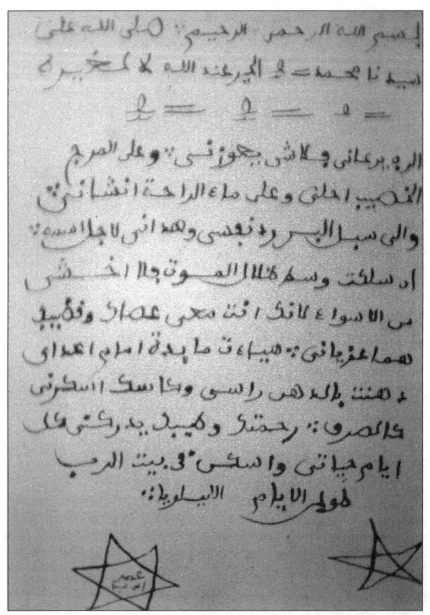

Fig. 32. The Bismillah, 23rd Psalm, and Quranic phrase "All good is from Allah, and no other."

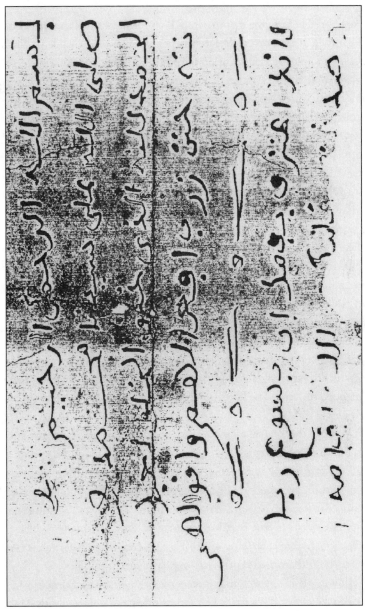

Fig 33. The Bismillah and "This is How You Pray, You. . . ." Both
from Eliza H. Owen Scrapbook.

As I noted before, the manuscript fell out of sight until the winter of 1995. In December, it and several related papers, mentioned earlier in Chapter 6, were shown to me for identification purposes, and they were auctioned off to the knowledgeable collector Derrick J. Beard, by Swann Galleries, New York. The present owner, interested in educating the world about Umar and his peers, has generously allowed me to tell about it and to print the accompanying photo. It is sewn into light brown wrapping paper. On this cover, Fig. 34, someone has written, "The Life of Omar ben Saeed, called Morro, a Fullah Slave, in Fayetteville, N.C. owned by Governor Owen, Written by himself in 1831, & sent to Old Paul, or Lahmen Kebby, in New York in 1836, Presented to Theodore Dwight by Paul in 1836, Translated by Alex. Cotheal, Esq. 1848. (The beginning at the other end.)"

There are a few inaccuracies here, but the writer knew which end was up. The booklet has twenty-three pages, but writing appears only on fifteen. There is no writing on pages 6–13. As I write this sentence in April 1996, contemporary translators are at work on the manuscript once again. Thus far, however, no one has gone through it completely. Two who have begun translating it find the earlier translation close to the original, but one of these, Muhammad al-Ahari, insists that there is no negation of Islam or Muhammad in the original. As is also true in the Quran, there is an acceptance of the prayers and prophethood of Jesus. The latter acceptance appears to be added to the spiritual wealth Umar had been gathering for most of his years.

Following the Fatiha, a long *qutba*, lesson or sermon, opens the autobiography: Surah 67 complete. This Surah also closes the manuscript sent to Key, Fig. 23. The spiritual rather than the physical person is the usual subject of Muslim autobiographies. As I noted earlier, most of the Surah deals with the necessity for humans of right thinking about the power, creation, and true prophet of God. It is true that Muhammad is not named here—allowing the introduction, perhaps, of Jesus—but it is also true that this Surah is central to assertions of Muhammad's ultimate prophethood.

Following this *qutba*, Umar is as conventional as any European in apologizing too much for his writing; Umar says he has forgotten both Arabic and his own language (Fulfulde, written with Arabic letters). Then he proceeds, as any Muslim must with any serious action, with the Bismillah: "In the name of God, the Gracious, the Merciful." He tells most of his own life story as outlined before. When he gets to his purchase by "Jim" [*sic*], apparently with the assistance of John Owen he expresses his gratitude for the life they have allowed him: "These men are good men. What food they eat they give me to eat. As they clothe themselves they clothe me." This was treatment that Africans expected when they adopted a master's religion—as was the way in Muslim lands and supposedly also in lands enlightened by the New Testament, though it was seldom the case, according to ar-Rahman, other American slave narrators, and histories of American treatment of Africans.

Umar then stretches: "They permit me to read the gospel of God, our Lord, and Saviour, and King"—the New Testament God, presumably. But this god is seen in a Quranic way as one "who regulates all our circumstances, our health and wealth, and who bestows his mercies willingly, not by constraint." The translator has Umar speaking of "Lord Jesus the Messiah" as God. It is not likely that even a converted Muslim would go this far toward a trinitarian belief.

Another section tells what Umar used to do as a proper Muslim back in Africa. He followed the Five Pillars. This section concludes with "Written A.D. 1831."

Then the translation suggests a second beginning. Umar must have been convinced that he should be more direct in his gratitude. There is no Surah from the Quran; instead, this section begins with a list of sixteen Owen family members and is followed by Umar saying that he has gone from taking pleasure in the Quran to finding it in the "gospel" of "Jesus the Messiah." Some of his language ("Lord of all worlds") suggests that he has the same god in mind on either side of his ostensible conversion, but the translator has Umar declaring that he has dropped the Fatiha for "Our Father, . . ." (the Lord's Prayer), "in the words of our Lord Jesus the Messiah." These words are unequivocal—but were also available only in translation, and Umar may have felt he had to say something like this to keep in the good graces of the Owens. This notion is borne out by Umar's 1857 piece.

Umar's autobiography included two final paragraphs: details about the abuse he had suffered in Africa, where "wicked men took me by violence," and in Charleston, where "I fell into the hands of a small, weak and wicked man, who feared not God at all, nor did he read (the gospel) at all nor pray"; and how he ran from this wicked man to North Carolina and the good Owens. A final paragraph makes it clear that Umar is very happy that he is being treated well by the Owens and is not required to do "hard work."

We await a definitive translation—and the discovery of more of Umar's papers.

There are, finally, two interesting sidelights on Umar ibn Said's history. One account of him said that Umar received a letter in Arabic from a man named Yang, a Muslim from Canton, China. Apparently a missionary had brought one of Umar's letters to Yang, who was moved to respond in kind. Nothing more

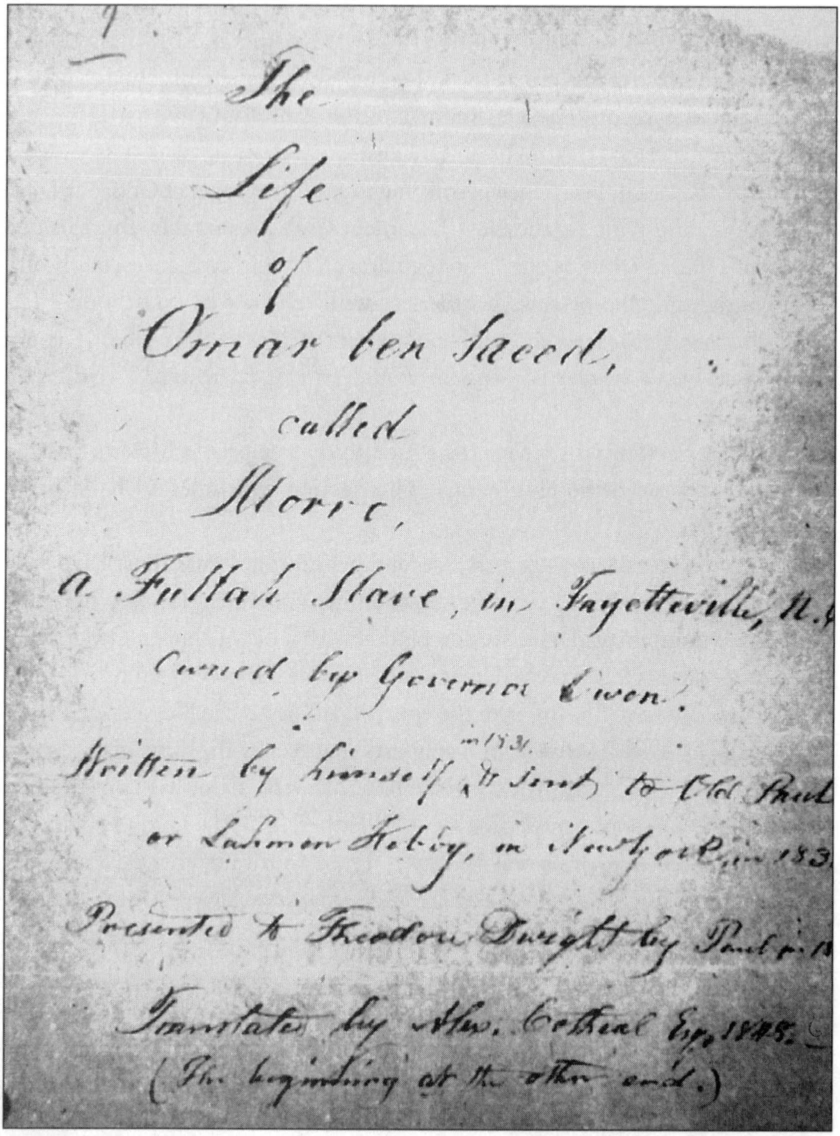

The

Life

of

Omar ben Saeed,

called

Morre,

a Fullah Slave, in Fayetteville, N.C.

Owned by Governor Owen.

Written by himself in 1831 & sent to Old Paul

or Lahmen Kebby, in New York in 1836

Presented to Theodore Dwight by Paul in 1836

Translated by Alex. Cotheal Esq, 1848.

(The beginning at the other end.)

Figs. 34 & 35. Cover Page and First Page of Umar's "Life." Photos courtesy of Derrick Joshua Beard.

بسم الله الرحمن الرحيم صلى الله على سيدنا
محمد تبرك الذي بيده الملك وهو على كل
شيء قدير الذي خلق الموت والحياة ليبلوكم
ايكم احسن عملا وهو العظيم العزيز الغفور
الذي خلق سبع سموات طباقا ما ترى في خلق
الرحمن من تفاوت فارجع البصر هل ترى من
فطور ثم ارجع البصر كرتين ينقلب اليك
البصر خاسئا وهو حسير ولقد زينا
السماء الدنيا بمصابيح وجعلناها رجوما
للشياطين واعتدنا لهم عذاب السعير
وللذين كفروا بربهم عذاب جهنم وبئس
المصير اذا القوا فيها سمعوا لها شهيقا وهي

seems to have come of this correspondence, but other letters by Umar were shown by Lamine Kebe's biographer to Rev. Daniel Bliss, president of the Syria Protestant College. Bliss followed up on what had been learned from Lamine Kebe, as well as what had been heard and read of Umar, by sending a case of Bibles in Arabic to Liberia to be distributed around Umar's distant country.

This act provided, in fact, an opening into the Muslim hinterland for the young Arabic studies program of the College of Liberia and for its founder, the great black Caribbean scholar Edward Wilmot Blyden, who began teaching Arabic in Liberia in 1867—as I mentioned in the conclusion to Chapter 6.

SELECTED READINGS

"Autobiography of Omar ibn Said, Slave in North Carolina, 1831," *American Historical Review*, XXX, No. 4 (July 1925), 787–795.

Gregory Townshend Bedell, "Prince Moro," *Christian Advocate* (July 1825), 306–307.

George H. Calcott, "Omar ibn Said, a Slave Who Wrote an Autobiography in Arabic," *Journal of Negro History,* 39 (1954), 58–63.

Philip D. Curtin *Economic Change in Pre-Colonial Africa* (Madison: University of Wisconsin, 1975).

Theodore Dwight, Jr., "Condition and Character of Negroes in Africa," *Methodist Quarterly Reviw* (Jan. 1864), 77–90.

John F. Foard, *North America and Africa*, 3rd. ed. (Statesville, N.C., 1904).

Mathew B. Grier, "Uncle Moreau," *African Repository* (June 1869), 174–176.

Ralph R. Gurley, "Secretary's Report," *African Repository*, XIII (July 1837), 201.5

Margaret McMahon, "Bladen Slave was also a Prince," Fayetteville *News and Observer* (17 March 1968).

On Futa Toro in Umar's day, see Gaspard Mollien, *Travels in the Interior of Africa to the Sources of the Senegal and Gambia* (1820) (reprinted London: Cass, 1967).

Louis T. Moore, "Prince of Arabia," Greensboro *Daily News*, 13 February 1927.

William S. Plummer, "Meroh, a Native African," New York *Observer* (8 Jan. 1863).

George E. Post, "Arabic-Speaking Negro Mohammedans in Africa," *African Repository* (May 1869), 129–133.

[Henry M. Schieffelin], *People of Africa* (New York: Anson D. F. Randolph, 1871).

Clyde-Ahmad Winters, "*Roots* and Islam in Slave America," *Al-Ittihad* (Oct.–Nov., 1976).

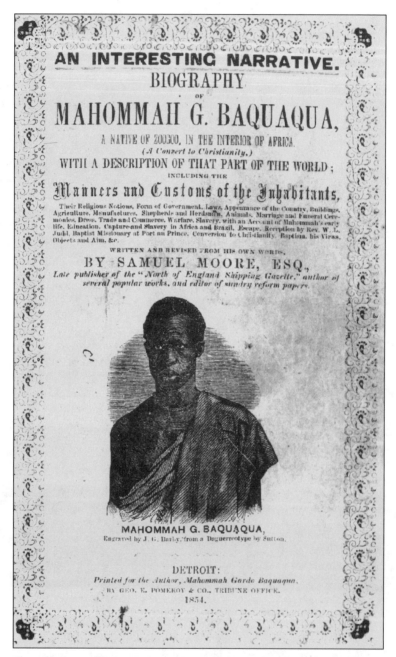

Fig. 36. Cover of Mahommah G. Baquaqua's *Biography*, Detroit, 1854, Burton Historical Collection, Detroit Public Library.

8

The Transatlantic Trials
of Mahommah Gardo Baquaqua

Mahommah Gardo Baquaqua was an unambitious, undisciplined, modestly intelligent boy and man who loved his mother, liked alcohol, and got in trouble out of mischief or boredom rather than malice—a not-unusual case on any continent. But this young African's troubles led him a long way from home. He was born around 1830 in Djougou, a large city in present-day Benin. Uninterested in school and religion, his father's and older brother's rigorous Islam, or physical labor, Baquaqua became a victim of others at home and abroad. He was captured during a distant war and was released; became a petty servant of a petty non-Muslim chief; was tricked by drinking friends into slavery; was marched toward the coast by male and female purchasers; suffered a long passage across the sea; and was owned by a harsh baker and then a cruel shipmaster and his wife in Brazil. He was a mistreated steward and near alcoholic on board a ship that sailed to New York City; a lonely fugitive there and in Boston; an uneasy convert to Christianity in Haiti; a mistreated student and a dubious missionary candidate in upstate New York and in Canada; a published storyteller in Detroit, Michigan, in 1854; and in 1857, a sojourner in England on his way, he hoped, home to Africa.

There are several uncommon elements beyond the obviously unusual geographical and biographical aspects of Baquaqua's life story. His *An Interesting Narrative. Biography of Mahommah G. Baquaqua* is the only known description of that time by an African of his homeland and its neighbors. Its section on his life in Brazil is the only known slave narrative from that time and nation. Its pages on his escape in New York City offer glimpses of a secretive "undersea railroad" that rescued victims of slavery in Northern seaports. Its personal account of U.S. missionaries in Haiti provides an uncommon African viewpoint. And its black student's description of the only pre–Civil War American college to boast African American professors—although he does not mention any of the three directly—is, so far, unique.

By 1854, Baquaqua had gained enough attention to become noticed in several American newspapers and magazines, according to a short account of Baquaqua in *Facts for Baptist Churches* (Utica, 1850) that provides one of two known portraits of him (Fig. 37). Presumably, several of these undiscovered articles will be found one day. There are also letters to and from Baquaqua yet to be found. To date, I have found seven letters in English in his own hand written in 1853 and 1854. These show that Baquaqua was seeking a way to go home to Africa as a missionary, teacher, or cook. They also show that he was unprepared religiously, intellectually, or emotionally for any of these positions. Still, he did get to England somehow.

When his overtures to American missionary societies seemed to have failed, Baquaqua convinced himself that it might be helpful to his pocket and proposals to tell his story in print. He found a willing and helpful publisher for his sixty-five-page *Biography of Mahommah Gardo Baquaqua*, composed with the aid of a collaborator about as naive as himself. On the title page, Samuel Downing Moore claimed previous editorial and professional writing experience, but there is little evidence of that in the text. In his "Preface and Compiler's Notes," Moore said that Baquaqua spoke "imperfect English" but that their book would be readable, clear, instructive, plain spoken, amusing, and helpful to "all classes of readers" and to Baquaqua's missionary project. In places the text is all of these things, but it is usually disorganized and incomplete on its many topics and is too often directed toward young people rather than adults capable of forwarding Baquaqua's religious career. Further, Moore's introductory paragraphs show that he was absolutely ignorant of and overly sentimental about Africa and simplistically Eurocentric in his interpretations of Baquaqua's words and motivations for returning to Africa. On the other hand, the naïveté of both men makes much of this text fascinating for its directness and its unresolved two-part structure. Although it begins as biography, about a third of the way through it becomes autobiography. The title page includes the phrase: "Written and revised from his [Baquaqua's] own words." Baquaqua promised a fuller version later.

Fig. 37. Mahommah Baquaqua and Missionary William L. Judd, c. 1848, from Andrew T. Foss and E. Mathews, *Facts for Baptist Churches*, 1850. Miller Library, Colby College, Waterville, Maine.

The *Biography* is very strangely organized. It opens with a sign of the writer's naïveté: a list of the numbers from one to one thousand in the language of the Songhai—Baquaqua's father's people. Some pages later Baquaqua takes pride in having learned these numbers in Portuguese. Baquaqua apparently believed that such a recitation would show his intelligence and recommend his cause. Moore's placement of this list suggests that he agreed. One-third of what follows is divided into six short chapters made up of haphazard, usually unreliable notes on Baquaqua's native Islam, government, scenery, agriculture, people, manners, official ceremonies, trade, wars, and slavery, while a seventh chapter, taking up the last two-thirds of the document, finally delivers Baquaqua's unvarnished life tale.

I will emphasize the latter too. Baquaqua was born into a family with fading fortunes on the paternal side, saved by the rising fortunes of the single wife his father could afford. His father was a "not very dark complexioned," devout Muslim whose people had been called Songhai until they were dispersed after the fall of their extensive empire by the capture of their capital, Timbuktu, by Moroccan and Portuguese mercenaries carrying firearms—never before seen in the interior of Africa in 1591. His father was born in "Berzoo" (Borgu), where the displaced Songhai were called Dendi. Baquaqua's mother was a Hausa woman from the city of Katsina (as was the mother of Abu Bakr, Chapter 2; Katsina was also where Mohammed Ali ben Said was taken after his capture— see Chapter 9).

Baquaqua was born in the large city of "Zoozoo" (Djougou), a walled city unvisited by Europeans until after 1854. The city was a trading center on a major route between Kumasi to the west, the Ashanti capital in control of kola, salt, metals including gold, European goods, and other items, and by the Hausa of Kano to the east, famous for their horses, donkeys, leather, ivory, cloth, and metalwork (see Chapter 1, Map 1). Rice and other grains, yams, fruits, beans, onions, cotton, and domestic and wild animals were plentiful.

Although Djougou's sizable Muslim population did not yet have its own mosque and held its prayers outside when Baquaqua lived there, Dendi Muslims got along well with Bariba, or non-Muslim, sections of town, and their *sarra* feast after Ramadan's month of fasting was celebrated by the Bariba ruler. Baquaqua represented it as a pleasant homeland, and his account accords with descriptions of nearby cities to the south explored by Englishman John Duncan's expedition in 1845–1846.

His father wanted Baquaqua to become as religious as his older brother, who became a teacher, adviser, and diplomat for distant non-Muslim chiefs as well as a supplier of Quranic amulets for ordinary people feeling a need for something to ward off evil. But Baquaqua decided at some point in his education that he was not interested in going further. He was apparently well protected by his mother against the father and brother. Moore ascribed Baquaqua's later recklessness to this maternal fondness.

For a while he was apprenticed to his blacksmith uncle, working in iron, copper, and brass. The uncle, Baquaqua said, worked gold and silver into bracelets, earrings, and rings. When the uncle died, Baquaqua's mother inherited his wealth. She soon needed it. She ransomed the older brother from captivity in a war to the east and later sent Baquaqua on a seventeen-day march to carry grain to his brother, then in Daboya to the west, where he was again an adviser to a king. Here both brothers got in the way of another war: "The guns began to boom away," Baquaqua said. Everyone fled for their lives, but the brothers were captured and led into a forest, where Baquaqua or Moore described the mosquitoes as more vicious than men: "real big hungry fellows, . . . they came whim! whim! about our ears, . . . I never wish to be in that place again"—suggesting a boyish narrator. This time his brother found an escape and ransomed Baquaqua.

His mother then helped Baquaqua obtain a messenger's position for a local king to whom she was related. Baquaqua described this position as the third most important post in service to a respectable king. As he tells about his duties, however, he appears to be a thug working for a thug. He ran with soldiers who, in lieu of pay, "plundered for a living." Often they did so under the influence of palm wine—and here Baquaqua acquired the predilection for alcohol that got him into many of his later difficulties. Petty chiefs and uncontrolled bands of young men such as Baquaqua unhesitatingly described did rise with the decline of the Borgu part of the old kingdom of Oyo (a loosely knit confederation of nearly autonomous peoples, including Yorubans, who were just becoming numerous in the Atlantic slave trade).

Around 1846 he was on his way back to Djougou to visit his mother when some supposed friends hired praise-singers to flatter Baquaqua, got him drunk, and took him to a great party, from which he awakened the next day to discover himself a prisoner and a slave. He cried for his mother and drank some more. He was put into a rough wooden collar, and his march to the sea—more than three hundred miles away—began. He described passing friends unable to rescue him and his sale to a female slave trader, who carried him farther south for "several" days past towns, great prairies with very tall grasses, and some mountains where the weather was very pleasant.

At a town called Efau, Baquaqua was sold to a rich man. He was "very well treated" but did not like the work assigned to him and threatened to run away. After "several weeks" there, he was led past fearsome leopards and other wild animals further south to Abomey, the capital city of the Dahomeans, famous for its female armies and the king's house decorated with the skulls of enemies. Baquaqua saw one of the warrior-wives but missed the house. He seems to have been more interested in the city's reputation as "a great place for whiskey." At this point he gave up hope of seeing his mother again.

A day and a half below Abomey—which Baquaqua called Dohama—he saw his first white man and his glass windows. Baquaqua said that the man "took my attention very much." More importantly, he also saw an acquaintance who had disappeared from Djougou two years earlier. He too had been kidnapped and enslaved. They were unable to help one another. Two nights and a day's ride down a river led to "a very beautiful place"—an ironic touch—where he was confined in a slave pen, branded with a hot iron, bound in chains or ropes, and saw the seashore and a waiting European ship.

This last sight was terrifying. Baquaqua thought the ship might be a white man's "object of worship" or a place where the waiting captives were to be slaughtered. The prisoners—"from all parts of the country"—had been given a kind of feast before boats took them to the waiting ship. Those rowing had been given a lot of whiskey. One of several crowded boats did not make it through a rough sea; it capsized and all but one of thirty aboard drowned. Baquaqua, of course, was in another boat that did make it. He said everyone was naked; males and females were separated; the hold was too low to stand in; and the loathesomeness and filth—probably not Baquaqua's exact words—were horrible. All suffered from seasickness early on. The only food was "corn [grain] soaked and boiled." A pint of water per day was insufficient but was all he was given. Only twice in what was commonly at least a six-week voyage was he allowed to go on deck; many of his fellow captives died.

Finally, Pernambuco in northern Brazil was sighted. For a day there was no food, water, or noise allowed. The slave trade was not yet illegal there but was apparently frowned upon. At night the prisoners—who had been "viewed and handled" by potential buyers visiting the ship—were taken ashore to a trader who liked using the whip. On the ship there had been some Africans—apparently crew members—who sometimes talked to the captives and who spoke Portuguese. Baquaqua had begun to practice their talk and found his little knowledge useful to his eventual purchaser, a baker. Moore the Baptist and Baquaqua the one-time Muslim had some fun mocking his Portuguese master's Catholic images and religious services for the "benefit" of slaves. But Baquaqua learned that becoming Christian in Pernambuco did not mean becoming free.

After being forced to help build a stone house, Baquaqua tried to serve his master diligently and honestly as a bread seller. He even avoided drinking until he found that his master would not be pleased and could not lighten his load no matter how hard he worked. He tried running away but was caught. He decided to do little and to drink whiskey but was beaten for his lack of effort. He thought of killing his master but decided it would be easier to drown himself by jumping in a river. He found no luck that way; he was saved and was beaten severely.

Baquaqua was then sold to another cruel purchaser who abused his female slaves but who soon sent Baquaqua off to Rio de Janeiro, where he was sold to a sea captain. In that service, he rose from brass polisher to understeward and steward but had a hard time pleasing the captain's Brazilian "lady," who was often angry, apparently because she had been kidnapped by the captain as she was about to be married to another man. Several exciting episodes at sea suggest that the captain's seamanship was less than perfect. Baquaqua was also treated harshly by the ship's mate, against whom he once raised his arm to fight back. The captain's brutal punishment was stopped by the capricious "wife." At another time, in port, Baquaqua's drunkenness led to a ducking and presumably another beating.

His last voyage with the captain—carrying coffee to New York City about two years after he was taken from Africa—brought Baquaqua to freedom. But his escape was not easy. He and other slaves had heard that slavery did not exist where they were heading. He had high hopes of escaping, did not want to appear unhappy about his situation, and obeyed all orders to the letter. But a hurricane and his captain's anger at his inability to light a signal lamp led to a severe beating that endangered his life as well as his hopes. Baquaqua refused to beg for mercy as demanded and tried to fight back. He was locked up, became sick, and nearly despaired.

But an Englishman on board encouraged Baquaqua with stories, in Portuguese, of New York and freedom and taught him the English word "free." Once he reached port, a local pilot was positively decent to him, and on the second day a committee of African Americans somehow got on the ship and boldly inquired about the presence of slaves aboard. These people were undoubtedly members of the New York Vigilance Society, which had recently been revived, going about business similar to their earlier rescues of slaves from visiting ships. Baquaqua, another young male, and two female slaves understood what was being asked but did not know how to act. Shortly thereafter, Baquaqua recklessly declared that he would soon be free and was again locked up.

After "several" days, however, Baquaqua broke out, jumped ship, and ran for his life. He was captured by authorities and returned to the ship, but by then New York lawyers had been informed of his situation, presumably by the Vigilance Society, and a few days later Baquaqua was taken off the ship, carried to City Hall, and brought to hearings, held in prison, brought to hearings again—

proceedings he could not possibly understand—until he was physically rescued by "friends" who were undoubtedly from or related to the Vigilance Society again. In 1848, probably around the age of twenty—here the *Biography* is unhelpful—Baquaqua was a free man. His new friends helped him and a fellow fugitive from the ship flee to Boston, where they were taken care of for about four weeks before someone decided they needed to fly farther. Given the choice of England or Haiti, Baquaqua seems to have concluded that the climate and color of people in Haiti would be more agreeable, and there the two were sent.

On the way to Haiti, a colored man named Jones took an interest in Baquaqua and started teaching him about shadows and other common folkloric phenomena. In Port au Prince, Haiti's capital, Baquaqua felt free but had difficulty because he did not know the language. A military officer was helpful but offered little more than shelter and whiskey. A black man from America proved to be a mean employer; Baquaqua and his companion suffered from malnutrition and fell ill. His companion found out about a Baptist missionary from the military officer, who probably thought he could take care of two pests at the same time and who sent Baquaqua to the missionary for help.

William L. Judd, his wife, and the latter's sister were the first missionaries from the United States to work in Haiti. They had been sent by the American Free Baptists, who were strongly antislavery and, according to two of the organization's leaders, were dismayed by the carelessness with which U.S. Christians had treated the Haitians, who were the second American people to declare themselves free of European rule and who had fought heroically to gain their eventual independence in 1804. But Haitians were also black. Their country, its rights, and its people's needs in the form of trade were not recognized by the United States until the Civil War.

When the Judds arrived in Haiti in January 1847, they were hardly welcomed by the nominally Catholic nation. But by October, Judd was able to baptize twenty-four natives. In 1849 he also baptized Mahommah Baquaqua, declaring that this man's baptism was an unusually affecting moment. Judd wrote, "[Baquaqua] is endowed by nature with a soul so noble that he grasps the whole world at a stroke, in the movement of his benevolent feelings. . . . He now seems filled with the most ardent desire to labor for the salvation of souls. . . . 'I want to do all for God, all for good,'" Baquaqua reportedly declared. Characteristically inconsistent—and candid—he also said he wanted to go back home to Katsina to visit his mother.

The relationship between Judd and Baquaqua undoubtedly often reflected the portrait of the two men accompanying this chapter. Baquaqua must often have appeared as cowed and Judd as tired as this image suggests. Baquaqua was an imperfect candidate for conversion. He says he tried to be good but was often unkind, even to the saintly Mrs. Judd: "I must confess, I sometimes treated them rather badly. I had not much gratitude then. I would often get very drunk and be abusive to them, but they overlooked my bad behavior always, and when Mrs. Judd would try to coax me to go home and behave myself, I would fight her and tell her I would not."

After his conversion, Baquaqua declared that he would give up alcohol completely. The Judds apparently had some hopes that he was sincere, and he accompanied Mrs. Judd to upstate New York for her to visit her family and for Baquaqua to become educated in preparation for a missionary life. Threatening storms at sea and a visit to their ship in a Southern port by a slave trader who wanted to buy Baquaqua did not interrupt their long voyage. Nor was it stopped by a racist sailor who tried to cause trouble until Baquaqua "let him see a little of my own ugliness." Shortly after arriving in New York City again, on a boat on the Erie Canal, Baquaqua became playful and thought of pretending to be a fugitive slave. He had to be shamed into admitting that he was Mahommah Baquaqua from Haiti.

In about a month, he was settled into the academy, or "primary department," of Central College in McGrawville, New York, sponsored by the American Free Baptist Missionary Society. It was the only college in the United States that knowingly hired African American professors before the Civil War— and one of few to have women as faculty. Central College included three mulattoes who clearly identified themselves as "black." Charles L. Reason, professor of belles lettres (literature), and French and adjunct professor of mathematics, 1849–1850, was later an important educator in New York City. William G. Allen, professor of Greek and German, 1850–1853, got into trouble at Central when he not only fell in love with Mary King—one of Baquaqua's student teachers and a mature daughter of liberal whites—but when the two seriously considered marriage. There was a near riot, virtual imprisonment of Mary King, and an escape and elopement not unlike Othello's, perhaps, but followed by a hasty retreat to England in 1853. Miss King composed a poem on Baquaqua that was reprinted in the *Biography*. (Coincidentally, one of Baquaqua's letters offers a defense against an allegation that Baquaqua was also trying to "marry" a white student later in 1853. The woman's parents and classmates probably feared an affair rather than a marriage.) The third African American professor, George B. Vashon from Pittsburgh, had been a professor at Haiti's College Faustin between January 1848 and the summer of 1850. He became a professor of classics at Central College from 1854–1857—too late to share impressions of Haiti with Baquaqua.

Baquaqua's three years in and around McGrawville were hardly easy. He had to do manual labor for his keep; he was regularly harassed by white students; and he probably was not ready to be a student or sojourner there. He quietly put up with many of the tricks other students pulled, but he left the college for a while to study privately with American Free Baptist missionaries and at a school at nearby Freetown Corner. His biography says that at some point he returned to the college but left to visit Canada, where he was treated so well by everyone that he eventually moved there to became a naturalized citizen.

The *Biography* ends with a suddenly remembered hope for help to come to Baquaqua so that he might return to his own country as a missionary. But all assertions about Baquaqua's Christian conversion and zeal came not from Baquaqua but from Judd or Moore. Readers seeking reasons to support this man as a missionary could not have been satisfied by what is said about his religious and educational preparedness. Nor was there any help in the otherwise pleasing addition of a strongly abolitionist but weakly Christian poem supplied anonymously by James Monroe Whitfield, an African American whose emigrationist arguments against Frederick Douglass and others were printed in Detroit by the same printer who published Baquaqua's work.

More may be learned about these last known incidents of Baquaqua's life from Baquaqua's seven extant letters. These show that as late as the summer of 1853, he was nowhere near being a religious scholar. He had learned how to write an understandable letter, although he confused tenses and long and short vowels. In August 1853, at a low point in his relations with New Yorkers and amid some difficulty with his original Free Baptist sponsors, perhaps, he wrote to George Whipple, the secretary of the nonsectarian American Missionary Society of the Congregational Church. He said he would not tell others about their correspondence but would like to go home soon—very soon. He wrote, "I made my mand [*sic*] to go to Africa this fall, if I can. . . . I feel I may do more good in Africa than I can here." He added that he believed in one Church. This bland statement could not have made Whipple very hopeful about Baquaqua's evangelical zeal.

Baquaqua's second letter (September 14, 1853) was even more insistent in requesting a date for his return to Africa in October or December. The third was written to another correspondent; in it he admitted that he had been writing to Whipple because he thought he would not be allowed money that he thought was owed to him by some person or organization he does not specify in New York. He said he wanted to work with George Thompson, a famous missionary who had gone to Africa with Africans who were freed in a lengthy legal battle after their revolt on the *Amistad* slave ship hauled into New York in 1838.

On October 8, Baquaqua responded to a letter from Whipple. Baquaqua's letter indicates that he had been asked several serious questions. His statements and improved penmanship suggest that someone else was supplying some of the words and reminding Baquaqua to write more carefully. Baquaqua declared that nearby friends thought he would be acceptable for Thompson's Mendi Mission. He admitted that he needed more preparation and said that learning English was hard. Again, however, his missionary zeal is unconvincing because he added that he did not want to stay in the United States and wanted to go home. Nor was it helpful for him to write that he might go to Canada even though doing so might lead to his giving up on Africa—to say nothing of his giving up on converting Africans to Christianity. He thanked Whipple for his advice.

On October 26, Baquaqua had to respond to a more serious question. Whipple had been told that Baquaqua had been courting a certain young white lady. Baquaqua denied it; he said that they had met three years earlier and that she was nice but that he had not sought to marry her. Baquaqua wrote that local New Yorkers had seriously threatened him over the matter. Baquaqua had intented to go to a Freetown Baptist church to get a letter recommending him to a church in Canada, where he was planning to move. Someone warned him not to go because there was a rumor that he was going to the church to get married. Baquaqua wrote that he declared: "bless my body to day, Something I did not know nothing about it." Undoubtedly recalling the vicious crowds that had accosted Professor Allen only months earlier, Baquaqua did "give up going," as he feared they would do "very bad to me indeed." Subsequently, he felt he had to be very careful: "I dont go out much. I study my books, this all. I have a great trouble with these wickit people."

Following these words, Baquaqua wrote three words in Arabic, the language of his first school back home. They appear to be "Allah, Allah, most [or] ever," all that he could recall, perhaps, from the Bismallah: "In the name of Allah, most benevolent, ever-merciful." Perhaps he was thinking of going home and returning to his original religion. The orthography is similar in style to Nigerian manuscripts of the day. Baquaqua added a pathetic postscript that seems to show his doubts about being accepted as a missionary. In it he expressed a hope that his story would be told to Missionary Thompson for whom he said he would cook if he could not teach. He had become desperate to go back home.

Another letter to Whipple, January 6, 1854, still postmarked McGrawville, contained only five short, pessimistic sentences. It must have been written in a state of depression. He promised nothing and seemed to expect nothing: "Some thing which is nescessary for me to let you know. I should like to know, if I will go to Africa, this year or next year. Because I have to work in farms in the Spring, I board myself here about two years. I use to hire one acre of land. This reason I should like to know. Yours in Christian love, M. G. Baquaqua."

Later in the month, January 29, Baquaqua tried again. His studies helped make his next letter begin more formally: "Dear Br[other], Yours of the 14th is received. I now take my pen to address [?] you, . . ."

But the body of the letter is full of grammatical errors and logical or emotional confusion. He was again replying to the doubting Whipple. In short, Baquaqua declared that he was anxious to go to Africa to teach his countrymen because he believed he was a disciple of Christ since he too had suffered many trials. Setting aside any pretense of being a missionary, however, Baquaqua said he would like to be an interpreter of the Arabic and "Zogoo" languages, presumably Songhai. On that matter, he also said, unhelpfully, that he wished he understood English better.

Finally, Baquaqua responded to another Whipple statement: "You say that they [the Mission] want a good man to go there, but I did not know how good I am, but I love God and try to do which is right." Once again, Baquaqua is simple, direct, and unsure of both means and ends. There is also a postscript written in haste suggesting that Baquaqua is putting all his time into schoolwork. Again, the letter seems to be from a lonely and nearly desperate exile, and is still postmarked McGrawville.

That was Baquaqua's last letter, as far as I am aware, though there must be others elsewhere. At least momentarily, Mahommah G. Baquaqua must have felt proud and hopeful of good results when George A. Pomeroy, a sympathetic printer; Samuel Downing Moore, an interested fellow who claimed to be a writer; and J. G. Darby and Moses Sutton, local artists, combined to produce Baquaqua's book. It seems reasonable to think that he wrote one or two letters as his *Biography* was being composed and printed and that he wrote a few letters asking about sales and responses—or the want of any. It is pleasing to imagine that Baquaqua wrote some letters to tell someone about feeling safe and comfortable, at least temporarily, across the border in Canada. It is possible that he also wrote about meeting friendly missionaries or African colonizationists and finding a way to Africa, closer to his mother and his home.

Baquaqua did get as far as England by February 1857, according to an American Free Baptist Missionary Society correspondent (brought to my attention by Brazilian scholar Sylvia Lara). But the society declared that it would be a year before it would have any money to further his work. It is possible that Mahommah Baquaqua did get back home to Djougou, but after the disappointments he had experienced at the hands of Christians, he may have returned on his own, and, like the rest of the people in this book, reverted to the religion of his youth.

SELECTED READINGS

Baquaqua's letters are in Amistad Collection, American Missionary Association Papers, Tulane University, New Orleans.

Peter B. Clarke, *West Africa and Islam* (London: Edward Arnold, 1982).

John Duncan, *Travels in Western Africa in 1845 and 1846, Comprising a Journey from Whydah, through the Kingdom of Dahomey, to Adoofodia, in the Interior,* II (London: Bentley, 1847).

Nehemiah Levtzion, *Muslims and Chiefs in West Africa* (New York: Oxford University Press, 1968).

Samuel Moore, comp., *Biography of Mahommah G. Baquaqua* (Detroit, 1854). For full title see frontispiece.

Jane H. and William H. Pease, *They Who Would Be Free: Blacks Search for Freedom 1830–1861* (New York: Atheneum, 1974).

João José Reis, *Slave Rebellion in Brazil: The Muslim Uprising of 1835 in Bahia* (Baltimore: Johns Hopkins University Press, 1993).

For information about early academies for blacks, see Milton C. Sernett, *Abolition's Axe: Beriah Green, Oneida Institute, and the Black Freedom Struggle* (Syracuse, N.Y.: Syracuse University Press, 1986).

Fig. 38. Mohammed Ali or Nicholas Said, *Carte de Visite*, 1863? Massachusetts Historical Society, Boston.

9

Mohammed Ali ben Said, or Nicholas Said: His Travels on Five Continents

This chapter tells about an uncommonly bright, congenial, curious, and adaptable man whose people, the Kanuri; original name, Mohammed Ali ben Said; and references to Allah indicate his African Muslim beginnings. He did not forget the land and the religion of his fathers, as his autobiography shows, but by the time Said arrived in the New World in 1860, he had wandered so far and witnessed so much as both a slave and a freeman that his origins and religion were the oldest parts of his extraordinarily extensive multicultural baggage. The story of Mohammed Ali ben Said, or Nicholas Said, as he called himself after a problematic baptism in Russia, is by any standard an unusual one.

Said was born just west of Lake Chad (present-day Nigeria) into a prosperous military-merchant family around 1833. He was well educated but not wholly wise when he was captured by Tuareg raiders around 1849. Then his travels began. Said was marched as a slave across the Sahara Desert (a three-month trek), was sold in Tripoli and taken to Mecca, became a rich man's slave in Turkey, and was another rich man's servant in Russia and throughout Europe (1853–1859) before he was hired to be a manservant for a traveler to South and North America. Sometime in 1862, he became a teacher in Detroit, Michigan. A year later, Said joined the 55th Regiment of Massachusetts Colored Volunteers—as deserving of a movie as the more famous 54th, the subject of the film *Glory*. He was mustered out in South Carolina in the fall of 1865. Said married and then disappeared except for a barely legible handwritten note about his death, found in a copy of his regimental record held by the Massachusetts Historical Society, Boston: "Nicholas Said, Brownsville, Tenn. Aug. 6, 1882."

Before traces of him were lost, however, fellow soldiers admired Said as a pleasant person, sophisticated storyteller, and competent soldier. Thus far, a regimental record, two notes by people who knew him in the army, and a short article about him in a Groton, Connecticut, newspaper have been found. Each source provides corroboration of the facts and the character drawn directly in his own legacy: a remarkable photographic portrait and a charming and perceptive autobiography. The latter exhibits a number of subtleties: its African "father of his country" hero is nicely tailored to American sensibilities, and its Odyssean sensibilities and adventures speak to both American and European readers. Someone, probably Norwood P. Hallowell, a commanding officer who also spoke about Said elsewhere, apparently recognized these qualities and had the autobiography published in the most prestigious journal of the day, the *Atlantic Monthly*, under the title "A Native of Bornoo" (October 1867).

That Nicholas Said was not prevailed upon to produce a full-length book is a serious loss to mid-nineteenth-century comparative history. His observations during his extensive travels prove to be trustworthy, as most of his geographical and historical references can be confirmed elsewhere. His country, Bornu, had been the headquarters for two well-documented British exploratory expeditions in the 1820s and the 1850s, and the accounts of these groups square with Said's pictures of his homeland, its peoples, and the Saharan route north. Other works support his stories of subsequent travels. With genuine moral and fiscal encouragement, this obviously curious and well-read African could well have produced a multivolume *Travels on Five Continents* to balance bookshelves and points of view otherwise burdened only with multivolume *Travels* by Europeans.

What we have must do.

A headnote to Said's autobiography included these points:

> Nicholas Said, . . . was of medium height, somewhat slenderly built, with pleasing features, not of the extreme negro type [here Said's portrait, the frontispiece to this chapter, may be studied to figure out what the writer meant], complexion perfectly black, and quiet and unassuming address. Inquiry showed that he was more or less acquainted with seven different languages, in addition to his native tongue[s]; . . . At the request of those who had been from time to time entertained by the recital of portions of his history, he was

induced to put it in writing. The narrative which follows is condensed from
his manuscript, and his own language has been retained as far as possible.

How pleasing it would be to find Said's original manuscript.

The autobiography's title, "A Native of Bornoo," is inadequate for its
contents; I like to think that Said did not choose it. Said began with a traditional apology for possible shortcomings; but his cause was, of course, unusual: "Reader, you must excuse me for the mistakes which this article will contain,
as you will bear in mind that this language in which I am now trying to write
is not my mother tongue; on the other hand, I never had a teacher, nor ever was
at school for the purpose of acquiring the English. The only way I learned what
little of the language I know was through French books."

He began his story, however, with another tradition—the opening lines of
the majority of African American slave narratives: "I was born . . ." But his
own life story started far away "in the kingdom of Bornoo, in Soodan" (the
bilad as-Sudan, or land of the blacks in Arabic), which, he recognized, was
"imperfectly known." He described his land and that of the Fellatahs (Fulbe)
as being strong Muslim nations with high literary expectations for the upper
classes. His nation was the most civilized because of its trade with North African
states and those to the south in "gold-dust, ivory, &c.," a trade that included
slaves—a subject that is delicately omitted here. There have been varying opinions on the character but not the significant extent of Bornu's commerce.

These remarks led to a quite reliable historical sketch of Bornu's "romantic history" from the eleventh century to its near demise under the latest kings,
or *mais,* and the attacks from 1808 to 1815 of the Fula *jihad* led by a man Said
deprecatingly calls a shepherd, "Otman Danfodio." Usman Dan Fodio was one
of the most remarkably energetic, intelligent, literary, and successful Muslim
expansionists at a time when the rest of the Muslim world was being reduced
by European military advances. With only a little exaggeration, Said described
the temporary defeat of his people.

In 1815 Bornu regained its freedom by the efforts of an equally remarkable
leader, "Mohammed el Amin el Kanemy," whom Said called "the Washington
of Bornoo" (see Fig. 39). El Kanemy's victorious struggle, however, was spread
out over a longer period than the two months Said—or his editor's misread-
ing—alleged.

Like Washington, the successful liberator refused a crown; but he placed
himself at the disposal of the legitimate king. Here Said's story differs from
official histories given to the German traveler Heinrich Barth, but a similar

Fig. 39. Mohammed el Amin el Kanemy, Bornu's George Washington, from
Dixon Denham and Hugh Clapperton, *Narrative of Travels and Discoveries in Northern
and Central Africa in . . . 1822, 23, and 24,* 1826.

version has been found in Bornu folklore. This element provides another valuable aspect of Said's firsthand account. "Mais Barnoma" (Mai Dunama) grew
jealous of el Kanemy and involved the neighboring ruler of "Begharmi"
(Barghimi) in an elaborate plot to get rid of his enemy in a staged battle. With
foreknowledge of the trick from a messenger supposed to be reporting to
Dunama, el Kanemy rearranged the players, and in the end Dunama was killed
instead. Said wrote, "Allah, who protects the innocent and punishes the guilty,
was smiling over [el Kanemy]." The king of Barghimi was quickly defeated and
was forced to ford the Shary River, where many of his soldiers were killed. El
Kanemy then ruled securely for years, encouraging trade, defeating very hand-
some and very black enemies on Lake Chad (the Budduma), and absorbing
other lands and peoples until Bornu amounted to "nearly fifteen millions."

Said claimed that he was the son of Barca Gana, who was a slave but also
el Kanemy's premiere cavalry officer. This man became known in European
circles—as did el Kanemy, of course—when a British exploring expedition
penetrated the Sudan from North Africa (1822–1825). Barca Gana saved the
life of Major Dixon Denham, one of the expedition leaders. Said did not let on
that his father was a slave but claimed that both of his parents were from the
upper classes. Barca Gana, meaning a short man, was a common name; it is
not clear whether the famous cavalryman was Said's father.

Said was born in Kuka "a few years after the Waday war of 1831." At this
point, for some reason, perhaps editorial, national history is completely replaced
by Said's personal story. Said was one of "nineteen children, twelve boys and
seven girls. I was the ninth child of my mother." All his brothers were educated
in the Arabic and Turkish languages. Two of them were rich traders and had
been to Mecca as pilgrims. After his father's death, land and gold were set aside
to be distributed when he and others turned twenty, and Said was sent to school.
He must have been about seven then. In four and a half years he could read
and write Arabic and perhaps his own language using Arabic characters. He says
he could write both languages.

His age group—about three hundred boys around the age of twelve—
was circumcised and feted for fifteen days, according to custom. When he
returned home, "his mother, sisters, and brothers" treated him as "a pet for
some time." Four or five years later, Said wrote (around 1849), he and three
brothers were invited to the "very charming" "province of Yaoori and Laree
[Yo and Lari in Denham], . . . worthy to be called the garden of Eden." Denham
and Barth offered similar opinions. Here Said indulged a passion for hunting
in the woods that his mother had said would be his ruin. And so it was.

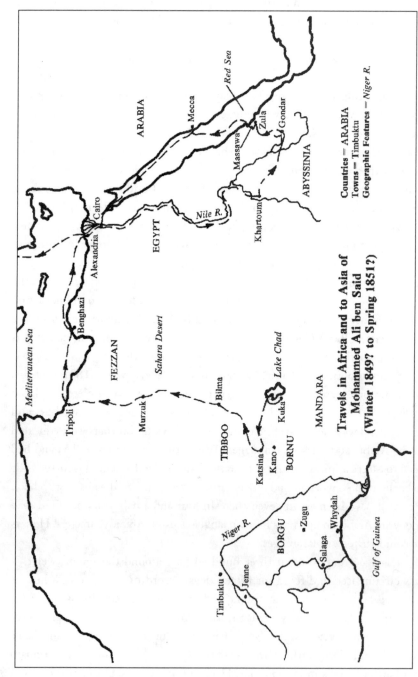

Map III. Travels in Africa and to Asia of Mohammed Ali ben Said.

Wandering Tuareg raiders, the "Kindil," as Said called them, took away eighteen of forty boys on horseback. Said cried for himself and for those he had persuaded to come into the forest with him. His particular odyssey had begun.

Said's route to North Africa and then to Arabia and Turkey may be followed in Map 3. His descriptions of the landscapes and people he met in Africa and across the Sahara—including a bespectacled Englishman in Murzuk—are similar to contemporary accounts by Barth and Barth's African servant Dorugu and are not very different from accounts of salt caravans and a journey through Ethiopia to Mecca in recent articles in *National Geographic*. Said did not stress the attendant horrors perpetrated by callous traders or the lusts directed against caravans made up of young women emphasized elsewhere. Instead, Said was interested in local stone formations, foods, and people—some of whom indulged in the use of hashish.

Said—one of five hundred trekkers in his caravan—was first the slave of an African-Arab carrying ivory and other goods. At Murzuk he was sold to someone who did not put him to work in the fields that he said he was not used to. He seems to have been a personal servant. He was sold again in Tripoli and commented on the variety of women he saw there, expressing his preference for Hausa women. His long trip as a slave to Mecca and back to Egypt led to another sale in Turkey to a man for whom all he had to do was tend his master's tobacco and pipes while fancily dressed. Said was shifted to this man's brother and then was sold in Constantinople to Prince Alexander S. Menshikov, the Russian general and chief envoy who, following the order of Czar Nicholas I, made demands on the Turks that neither they nor the British and French found acceptable. Shortly after Said and Menshikov left for St. Petersburg on May 21, 1853, the bloody Crimean War between these three powers and Russia began.

Said's new master, being rich, lived on the best street and in one of the better houses in the capital. But Menshikov was sent to the Crimea, and Said had trouble with the head servant and somehow managed to "engage service" with another prominent aristocrat, Nicholas Trubetzkoy. This man's country property included four villages and a house of marble as big as the Fifth Avenue Hotel in New York City, according to the well-traveled narrator. After about a year and a half in St. Petersburg, his master or employer—it is not clear which, except that Said said he was a personal servant—stood as his godfather and changed his name from Mohammed Ali ben Said to Nicholas Said when he was baptized on November 12, 1854 (Said wrote 1855, but the itinerary outlined later establishes the earlier date). Said reflected that he thought

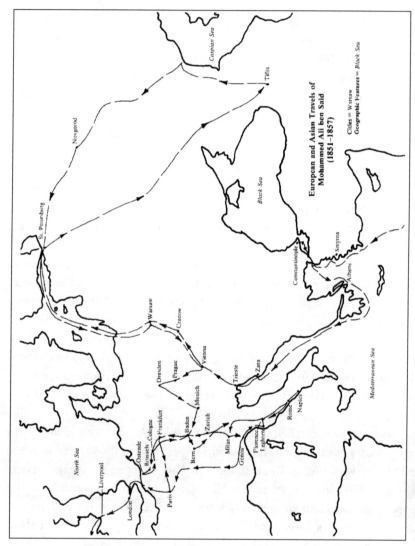

Map IV. European and Asian Travels of Mohammed Ali ben Said.

Trubetzkoy meant well, "but I cannot help thinking that the way I was baptized was not right, for I think that I ought to have known perfectly well the nature of the thing beforehand." He did not elaborate. Said's life was comfortable, but Trubetzkoy, who preferred "inaction" to any work, was a nervous wreck. Few Russians were comfortable under Czar Nicholas; Trubetzkoy's being the czar's godson apparently did not help him. He was not able to gain permission to travel to a Europe too liberal for the czar, but he and Said did go to Georgia in the Caucasus Mountains and on to Persia.

Czar Nicholas died in February 1855, and Alexander, his more liberal successor—who was to free his nation's serfs, or native slaves to the land, in 1861—allowed travel to the West. The two men set out almost immediately, and Said reported that Trubetzkoy's nervousness never appeared again. They vacationed back and forth across Europe for the next four years (see Map 4). In Dresden, Germany, he was bothered by children and adults who had never seen a black man or who were fascinated with his Asian "uniform." But he won over those who understood French (which he would have learned among the Russian aristocracy) with his stories and gifts. Better yet, Trubetzkoy's brother in Dresden gave Said several religious and secular books. He admitted that later, in Milan, Italy, "I did not behave as well as I might have done," as he drank and spent too much. But there he also met a countryman serving a Venetian marquis. At a party later in Florence, he thought he had a better time than did Trubetzkoy. At another, he met Prince Demidoff, who was notorious for mistreating his servants—and his wife, according to a contemporary source.

In the spring of 1856, Trubetzkoy and Said were in Paris; they spent the summer in London in the country, where Said concluded that English servants lived better than any others in Europe. He apparently shared their "gay times." Back in Germany, he served at an international soiree that included the rulers of Russia, France, and several German states as well as other foreign leaders. This meeting apparently led Nicholas Said "to think of the condition of Africa, . . . how European encroachments might be stopped, and her nationalities united." He wondered if the unification of the states in the New World might be a model; he wondered if he could induce several hundred young Africans to study in Europe; he cried when he thought of foreign superior weapons and tactics overcoming brave Africans. He prayed to Allah or the Russian Orthodox god—or perhaps both—to be of some help to his people.

But he was still in Europe. There was an interesting meeting with Trubetzkoy's beautiful niece, who was to marry the Duc de Morny; she hesitated but then allowed black Said to kiss her hand. In London again early in 1859,

Map V. The American Travels of Mohammed Ali ben Said.

Fig. 40. "Entrance of the Fifty-Fifth Massachusetts (Colored) Regiment into Charleston, Feb. 21, 1865" from Thomas Nast Engraving for *Harper's Weekly*.

Said, expressing his desire to do something for his country, and Trubetzkoy, professing that he would always be interested in Said's life, sadly separated. However, while Said waited for a ship to Africa, a "gentleman from Holland" proposed that Said should go with him to the United States and the West Indies. Having read much about these countries, he agreed and left Liverpool soon after New Year's Day, 1860. Map 5 touches on the main ports and places they visited. In Elmer, Ontario, Canada, his employer ran out of money. Said loaned the man $500, and they separated. Subsequently, Said's travels came to a temporary low point: "This failure [to get repaid?] compelled me to remain in this country and earn my living by work to which I was unaccustomed"— manual labor, undoubtedly, to which he had objected long ago in Murzuk.

As his editor reported, however, Said managed to avoid that terrible fate and convinced someone in Detroit that his English and education made him fit to teach school. A Union army recruiter saved him from that fate too when he signed Said up for the 55th Regiment of Massachusetts Colored Volunteers. According to a Groton (Connecticut) *Transcript* article that called Said's French "quite Parisian" and his Italian "correct," Said said he joined "because all his folks seemed to be doing so"—a nice identification with African Americans. The autobiography's editor barely touched upon Said's army days but did report that he rose to sergeant by July 1863 and later, in September 1864, asked to be reduced to corporal and to be detailed to a hospital in order to "acquire some knowledge of medicine." He added that Said was mustered out in South Carolina late in 1865 and concluded that a marriage, presumably with an American woman, might keep Nicholas Said from returning to Africa. The note on his death in Tennessee may be taken as corroboration of this guess, but thus far no information has been discovered on Said's movements from 1865 to 1882.

The regimental records of the Massachusetts 55th provide the dates given above and show Said enlisting in May 1863 and serving in Company I. Said may have requested hospital detail because of a desire to someday educate his native countrymen in the "sciences of the West," as he wrote in his autobiography. He may also have been attempting to do something about the woefully inadequate medical attention the 55th and all other African American regiments received.

Furthermore, although his regiment fought in important military battles (Ft. Mims and Honey Hill, 1864; James Island, Biggin Creek, S.C., 1865), its more serious and less well-known struggles consisted of its attempts to deal with the government's unfair treatment. In concert with the Massachusetts 54th Regiment, it waged a successful fourteen-month-long campaign for pay equal to that given white troops and a less successful one against extended fatigue duty beyond that required of white regiments. There were mutinies and near mutinies, but the poorer treatment continued. Still, the unhappy regiment had its moments of glory, when, for instance, it was in the vanguard of the Union troops that marched in to take Charleston near the war's close. The regiment was eventually mustered out on August 29, 1865. None of this military exercise and sordid treatment is included in Said's autobiography. His own sensitivity, perhaps, or his editor's sense of propriety may have led to this omission.

Another aspect of the man who began as Mohammed Ali ben Said may appear to have been omitted: his religion. But his autobiographical perspectives reflect Muslim training. Said asserts a lengthy history of Islam in his ancient country, and he declares that Allah protected Mohammed el Amin el Kanemy from Fellatah (Fulani or Fulbe) Muslims under the equally great leader Usman Dan Fodio in a protracted struggle—including slave-taking raids from both sides—over who was the most Islamically correct. Slavery is also a subject omitted in the autobiography.

Said took, however, longer than he should have to learn Arabic, and he did set out to picnic during Ramadan when he should have been fasting. Hence his capture, perhaps. His religion did not save him from being sold to several

Muslims, nor, since he did not go as a free person, did it allow him to visit the grave of Muhammad at Mecca—to complete, that is, the *hajj,* or holy pilgrimage. Possibly because of his audience, Said did not claim a strict adherence to Islam, and at least once he indulged in alcohol, which is denied to true believers. Perhaps he was simply being pragmatic, as he appeared to make himself comfortable with the religions of the powers around him: the Eastern Orthodox Church in Russia, Protestantism in Massachusetts, and possibly Roman Catholicism in Italy and France. Still, in his autobiography, his religious references were to Allah rather than Christ.

Since Said's *carte de visite* portrait and the Groton newspaper article were uncovered in 1994, it is pleasing to think that more might be found on this extraordinary man's life and career.

ADDENDUM: DECEMBER 2000

The chapter above begins and ends with the hope that more might be recovered of the writings and adventures of Mohammed or Nicholas Said. I am pleased that Routledge has allowed me to announce here the unusual and significant discovery of 228 very readable pages by this remarkable traveler and observer. With the assistance or direction of conservative Alabamans, Said published The *Autobiography of Nicholas Said: A Native of Bornou. Eastern Soudan, Central Africa* (Memphis: Shotwell & Co., Publishers, 1873). Its descriptions of varied landscapes, ethnicities, classes of people—including several historically noteworthy individuals—and the activities, architecture, and urban hygiene surrounding them, among more irregularly treated matters, are worthy of notice. That these emanate from an African makes them even more uncommon. Much of what appears in his longer work enlarges upon the twenty pages referred to above. Some details differ; some, but not all, are tweaked to better please conservative white Christians. Most unhappily, Said completely squelches his service in the Union Army, asserting that from 1858 to 1866 he moved around Europe. Surely a politic act for his time and place. Finally, Said's last chapter is an economic survival act: an extended advertisement on the delights of Bladen Springs, Alabama.

The *Autobiography* was brought to my attention by Harvard College graduate student Precious Muhammad, who is preparing an edition.

SELECTED READINGS

[Nicholas Said], "A Native of Bornoo,"*Atlantic Monthly* (October 1867), 485–495.

Allan D. Austin, "Mohammed Ali ben Said: Travels on Five Continents," *Contributions in Black Studies* 12 (1994), 129–158.

For a study of Said's homeland, see John Wright, *Libya, Chad and the Central Sahara* (Totowa, N.J.: Barnes and Noble, 1989).

For a report by early European visitors to Said's homeland, see Dixon Denham and Hugh Clapperton, *Narrative of Travels and Discoveries in Northern and Central Africa* (London, 1826) in *Missions to the Niger, II, III* (London: Hakluyt Society, 1966).

For a report by a contemporary European visitor, see Heinrich Barth, *Travels and Discoveries in North and Central Africa: Being a Journal of an Expedition Undertaken Under the Auspices of H. B. M. Government in the Years 1849–1855*, 3 vols. (1857–1858) (reprinted London: Cass, 1965).

For a study of el Kanemy's sophisticated Fula enemy, see Mervyn Hiskett, *The Sword of Truth: The Life and Times of the Shehu Usuman dan Fodio* (New York: Oxford University Press, 1973).

For a contemporary African's similar walk across the Sahara, see "The Life and Travels of Dorugu," trans. and ed. Paul Newman, in *West African Travels and Adventures: Two Autobiographical Narratives from Northern Nigeria* (New Haven: Yale University Press, 1971), 28–129.

For pictures of areas Said traveled early in his wanderings, see Victor Englebert, "I Joined a Sahara Salt Caravan," *National Geographic* (November 1965), 694–711.

For pictures of part of the route Said followed through Ethiopia to Mecca, see Owen Tweedy, "An Unbeliever Joins the Hadj," *National Geographic* 65 (June 1934), 761–789.

Allison Blakely, *Russia and the Negro: Blacks in Russian Thought and History* (Washington, D.C.: Howard University Press, 1986).

Mina Curtiss, "Some American Negroes in Russia in the Nineteenth Century," *Massachusetts Review* (Spring 1968), 268–296.

Charles B. Fox, *Record of the Services of the 55th Colored Regiment of Massachusetts Volunteer Infantry* (Cambridge, Mass.: John Wilson, 1868).

Index